Win With Your Money
From Negative Net Worth to Millionaire

Age 31 = -$99K

Age 32 = -$62K

Age 33 = -$48K

Age 34 = +$8K

Age 35 = +$78K

Age 36 = +$172K

Age 37 =+$330K

Age 38 = +$416K

Age 39 = +$670K

Age 40 = +$904K

Age 41 = +$1M

Cori Arnold

First published in 2023.

Copyright © Cori Arnold

Published by Cornball Productions LLC

Ohio, USA

Website: winwithyourmoney.com

Paperback ISBN: 979-8-218-27999-8

eBook ISBN: 979-8-218-28073-4

To my family for always being there.

Table of Contents

Introduction: Humble Beginnings

Section 1: Mindset: Enhance Your Awareness

1: You are the Common Denominator

2: Perspective Is Underrated

3: Figure Out Your Destination

Section 2: Regressive Debt: Get Your Hands Dirty

4: Debt has Non-financial Consequences

5: Compounding is Magical or Detrimental

6: Debt is a Puzzle to be Hacked

7: Let's Get Lean

Section 3: Retirement Investing: Create Your Ideal Life

8: You're Going to Stop Working Someday

9: Stick with Simplicity

10: Create Your Retirement Goal

Section 4: Progressive Debt: Balance Your Speed

11: Cash is King

12: Assets Make You Wealthy

13: Risk can be Healthy or Dumb

Section 5: Non-Retirement Investing: Reach for the Sky

14: The Next Lap

15: Accumulate Appreciating Assets

16: Stay the Course

Find your free budgeting, net worth, and debt tracker here:

https://winwithyourmoney.com/free-template

Introduction
Humble Beginnings

I felt this uneasy feeling the day I mustered up the courage to calculate my net worth for the first time. I had just finished the first year of a part-time MBA program, which was scheduled to last for two more years. My net worth was negative $83,423 and would only get worse. I had two more years of school and no cash to pay for it.

You would've thought this was my wake-up call. This should have been the red flag I needed to do something differently.

But, no, this didn't do it.

I felt bad about the situation. I felt uneasy about this knowledge, but I didn't change my behavior. I continued taking out loans for the MBA program and continued charging my credit cards like nothing was wrong.

...

I can happily tell you the outcome after I finally decided to make real changes. I went from having $260,000 of debt at age 31 to becoming debt-free five years later. I went from a net worth of negative $99,000 to becoming a millionaire 10 years later.

You might be thinking, *you inherited it, you married into money, or your parents gave it to you. This isn't realistic for everyone.* People have been brainwashed to think they can't do this, but I want to convince you that you can.

I didn't inherit a penny. I didn't marry into it. I came from a working-class family where the household income just exceeded the poverty threshold. We had food, but new clothes were almost always out of the question. Even though money was tight, my parents taught me great values, which were key to me becoming who I am today.

Growing up, the one luxury I got was an allowance. I could earn up to $5 each week. One week I earned $5 by raking the leaves of my parents' yard, which is about an acre in size. Can you imagine a 10-year-old raking an entire acre of leaves for $5? It took me most of that Saturday to complete. We joke about this today, but this hard work early in life cemented values in me that are irreplaceable.

I grew up in a small town with a population of 1,100 people. I wasn't supposed to accumulate wealth. I was supposed to be content working at a local job for 40 years. I was supposed to be satisfied making just enough to get by. However, I am not one to follow traditions.

My goal for this book is to inspire you to go on your own millionaire quest. Since you are reading this, I know you're on the right track. You have what it takes to do this. It's not going to be easy, but it will be worth it.

This is the first step – belief that it's possible.

Wrap your mind around it and believe it with all your being.

In ten years, I completely turned around my finances. This would have never happened if I hadn't shifted my mindset around money. Once I understood my out-of-control spending habits, my insane amount of interest expense, and my emotions with money, I was able to kickstart this journey.

The younger me was the person who didn't let her bank account get too large. When I had extra money, it was time to go shopping. I was this way for as long as I can remember.

In high school, for example, a few classmates and I helped our art teacher paint the exterior of his house. He paid us each $6 an hour and we worked for six hours. I had $36 to spend. My friend and I went straight to Walmart and blew it on who knows what, probably candy. Then, we went out to my car, and it wouldn't start. I was out of gas. I had no money since I had just spent it. I had to call my mom to come and get us. She wasn't happy.

As I got older, extra funds meant a trip to the mall. Even when I didn't have the money, if I felt like I needed something, then I simply went and purchased it, charging it to my credit card. I saw my credit card spending limit as something I could use freely. That line of credit was there for me to consume.

Quick trips to the store were no problem for me. Swipe. Done. Instant gratification. I did have the intelligence to know that I needed some money for payments, so I worked a couple small jobs in college, which amounted to ten-to-twelve hours per week. It was enough to get by. I wasn't worried about the growing credit card balances as I knew once I graduated college I would be working and receiving a regular paycheck. I thought, *how cool it's going to be when I receive a consistent paycheck. I won't have to worry about money ever again...* When you have money coming to you regularly, why would you need to worry about it?

I got approved for my first loan to buy an ATV (all-terrain vehicle aka four-wheeler) at age 23. I was so excited. My friend and I each got one, and we rode them almost every weekend. But, if you have a four-wheeler, then you need a truck to haul it, right? Of course, so I went ahead and got a truck. Yes, I took out another loan. At this time in my life, I was making $22,500 as an entry-level loan officer at a bank, and I was still living with my parents.

I was living the high life. I had a job. I went out every weekend. I was oblivious when it came to money, but from my perspective, things were good. Ignorance is bliss...

I was good until the bank hired another entry-level associate. This guy was a nice guy, but banking wasn't his forte. He read magazines at his desk, wasn't proactive, and wasn't trying very hard. They escorted him out one day and made the mistake of asking me to clear his desk. As I went through the pile of paper, I found one of his paychecks. He was my age, and they were paying him closer to $30,000, not $22,500 like me. I was instantly infuriated. They tried to appease me, saying he had more experience than me, but that wasn't good enough. It was time to figure out a new path.

Growing pains are always associated with learning, changed behavior, and bigger rewards. Learn to love growing pains, even though they can be difficult in the moment.

I quickly left the bank, briefly working as an accountant in Ohio, and within a year moved to Los Angeles. In LA I found a great job, working for a large company in finance. Getting this job was an adventure in itself. I started as a temporary contractor with no guarantees and assumed they weren't going to hire me because they'd interviewed so many people. However, I worked hard, and they eventually offered me the role.

My salary was much higher than it had ever been, but my expenses were higher too. At age 28, I asked my sister to borrow money for a bookcase I couldn't afford. I was starting an MBA program and had moved into a new apartment. My credit cards were maxed out on a laptop and new furniture. Looking back, I didn't need that bookcase.... Why couldn't I have seen this sooner? Why did a 28-year-old ask her 25-year-old sister for a loan? Why didn't I just wait until I had the funds?

If you haven't realized it, patience wasn't my forte.

I then went on to pursue my MBA, accumulating much more student loan debt. To top it off, I thought it was the right time to become a real estate investor during my first year at UCLA, so I purchased a duplex in Ohio without doing any research. To make matters worse, I used part of my student loans as the down payment for this property. Really smart... I ended up selling this property four years later for less than the original purchase price.

These are only a handful of the dumb decisions I've made with money. I could go on and on, but the point is if I can win with my money, then you can win with your money.

It doesn't matter what mistakes you've made. It doesn't matter how much debt you have. What matters is how strong your desire is to take back control.

Win with Your Money Stages

To win with your money, you must first understand what money is.

Money is only a tool. We can use it to our benefit, and we can use it to our detriment. On the benefits side, we can purchase healthy food, we can invest in appreciating assets, and we can help others. On the detriment side, we can buy drugs, we can blow it on stuff to impress others, and we can fund terrorists. I know these are extreme, but I want to make this point. Money is neutral. It's not bad or good; it's how we use it that creates the positive and negative outcomes in our lives.

When we make money's primary purpose to buy stuff we don't need, we are wasting a valuable resource. It's like cutting down trees for firewood. Sure, this is one purpose for trees, but it's not their primary purpose.

Trees create oxygen. If we didn't have oxygen, we couldn't breathe. Oxygen production is a much higher purpose of trees. In the same way, money has a higher purpose as well. Money provides security, freedom, and time. If you put your money in places where it will grow (aka: appreciating assets), then it will continue to provide benefits over your lifetime.

This book aims to give you a fresh perspective on money, while offering the tricks that work best. It is organized by these five stages of money:

1. Mindset: Enhance Your Awareness

2. Regressive Debt: Get Your Hands Dirty

3. Retirement Investing: Create Your Ideal Life

4. Progressive Debt: Balance Your Speed

5. Non-retirement Investing: Reach for the Sky

You have the power to take control of your money. By understanding these five stages, you will become the master of your money. You'll no longer live in the dark, controlled by your money. You'll realize you have the power to eliminate your debt, become a millionaire, and retire comfortably.

Mindset: Enhance Your Awareness

We have all been conditioned by beliefs from our past generations. If those generations weren't great with money, then you likely aren't great with money either. There is a high probability that you have the same deep-rooted beliefs as the people who raised you. Because these beliefs have been ingrained in you for many years, you've never questioned them.

Mindset is a lifetime journey that never ends. Being open to new beliefs puts you in the best position to become wealthy.

Regressive Debt: Get Your Hands Dirty

You may be asking yourself what regressive debt is. Regressive debt is similar to consumer debt, debt on your credit cards, vehicles, and other toys. Regressive debt is debt that literally takes you backwards. It is debt on depreciating assets – items that lose value.

You won't be surprised that the Regressive Debt stage is second. This stage represents the heightened focus on this type of debt until it's paid off. Bad debt is a burden. It's holding you back from investing to your full potential.

Retirement Investing: Create Your Ideal Life

Getting out of debt can take a long time. Because time is needed to maximize the impact of compounding, the Retirement Investing stage overlaps with the Regressive Debt stage. When you decide to start your money journey, it's time to start contributing to your retirement.

The sooner you start investing in your retirement, the better.

Progressive Debt: Balance Your Speed

Progressive debt is debt on appreciating assets. You may have heard this called 'good debt' in the past. I don't know if any debt is good, but some debt is beneficial in creating significant returns.

Think about your first house. Most people are not going to save up the entire purchase price. Instead, they'll save a down payment and borrow the remainder of it. The property you purchase is an appreciating asset. Its value increases over the long run, meaning you will most likely make a return on that property when you sell it.

Non-retirement Investing: Reach for the Sky

Non-retirement investing is any investment outside of your retirement accounts. This could be children's college funds, real estate, or a discount brokerage account. When you no longer have debt payments, you have extra money to invest.

This stage doesn't start until you're out of regressive debt completely.

Now, you may be asking, what if I already have regressive debt, progressive debt, and retirement accounts. That's perfectly fine. These are adaptive stages where you can start in multiple stages if that's where you are.

Later, you will see where I started my journey, drowning in regressive and progressive debt with a very flawed mindset.

In the following pages I describe the exact steps I took to eliminate my debt and to become a millionaire.

Section 1: Mindset
Enhance Your Awareness

Your mindset is the combination of your beliefs, thoughts, and attitude. These together influence your perspective.

We've all been conditioned by certain beliefs since childhood with regards to money.

Some common misconceptions are:

- You're going to work until you're eligible for Social Security.
- Investing in the stock market is gambling.
- Debt is normal.

If you continue to believe everything you've learnt from the broke people in your life, will you be surprised when you end up broke too?

Your deep-rooted beliefs, those beliefs you've had for years and decades, have been ingrained so deeply in your mind that you perceive them as facts.

Imagine this circle below is your mind. The grey half-circle represents your deep-rooted beliefs.

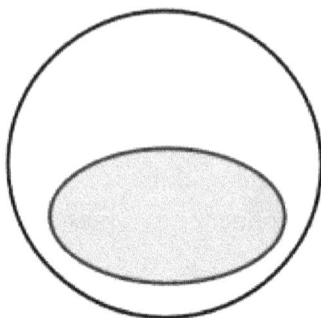

The longer you believe these beliefs, the more powerful they are in your life. An analogy I like to use is concrete. When you first pour fresh concrete, it's malleable. It's formless. Whatever form you build, it will mold into that shape.

This is similar to a thought you haven't quite converted into a belief yet. A thought is malleable. It doesn't have much power over you. However, the longer you hold onto that thought in your mind, the more likely it will turn into a belief.

As concrete cures, it becomes solid – very solid. In 30 days, it will become completely cured. You won't be able to crack it unless you use a tool. Similarly, as beliefs grow stronger over time, they become solid. They become facts in your mind, not easily broken and no longer questioned.

To break down these deep-rooted beliefs, it's time to start questioning them. The goal of this stage is to give you a toolset to break through your current beliefs.

The only way to change your financial future is to open your mind. Your mindset continues to be molded as you meet new people, read more books, and experience new things.

In some ways the Mindset stage is the most important stage. It may not have anything to do with numbers or accounts or balances, but without the right awareness, you won't be able to make any improvement in your money. You can take every financial action in this book, but if your mindset isn't open, then you'll never win with money.

1: You are the Common Denominator

We tend to think of our lives in silos. We have different aspects of our lives, different routines, different people, and different requirements for each silo. We carve out hours for our jobs, hours for our family and friends, and maybe an hour to exercise. We give each aspect a certain amount of energy each day based on our priorities.

We are in the center while our priorities make up the larger circle. We see each area compartmentalized and in its own space.

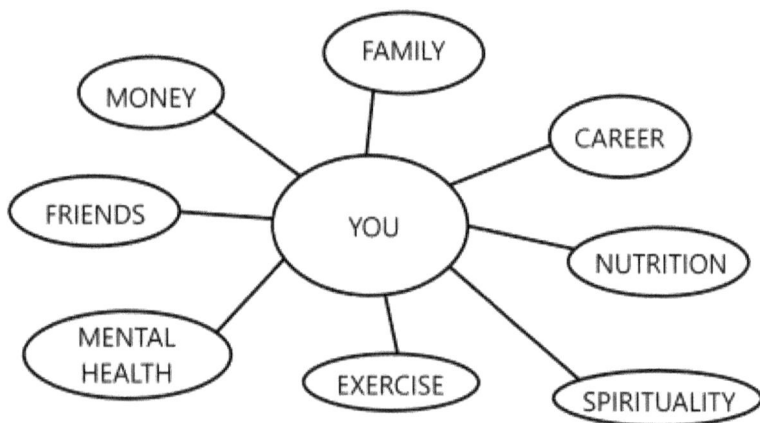

However, this isn't an accurate depiction. Even though we may see it like the above illustration, our silos are actually highly dependent on each other. We may separate aspects of our lives in our minds, but they really work together like this illustration below.

This illustration is messier, but this is reality. Everything in our lives is impacted by something else in our lives. They all overlap.

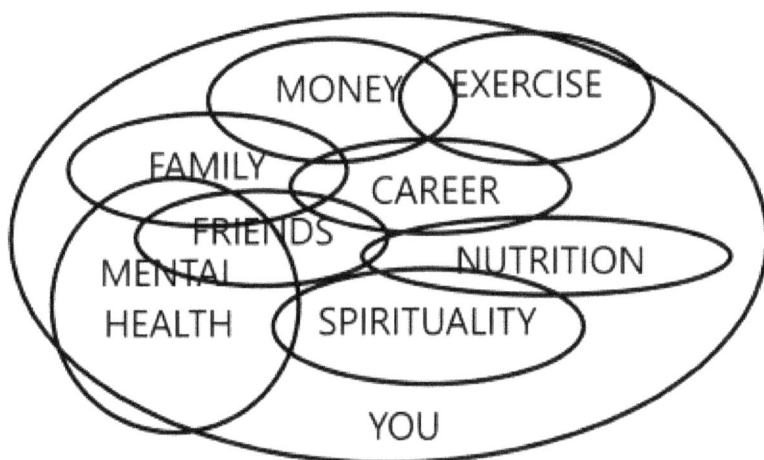

Change in one area influences changes in other areas. I used to watch the show, *The Biggest Loser*. In case you don't know the show, overweight contestants competed to lose the most weight. On one episode Suze Orman was the guest. Suze Orman is a financial expert who has written many best-selling books and had a television show for many years. Suze interviewed each of the participants and said she wasn't surprised that most of them had financial problems as well. She confirmed all aspects of our lives are connected.

When you are failing in one area, it's common for other areas to take that same trajectory. This is because you have one thing in common in all these areas. They are all controlled by you. You are the common denominator and create a web of interconnectedness in your life.

For example, if your health is decreasing, your job performance most likely will get worse. If you're stressed with money, that stress will carry over to your relationships.

This is why you can't push your money to the corner any longer. You can't avoid it.

Ignorance Isn't Bliss

Growing up, I loved the saying, *ignorance is bliss*. I thought what I didn't know couldn't hurt me. If I limited what I knew, I could live in my fairy tale life. How wrong was I?

My fondness of ignorance was verging on avoidance. Avoiding anything – feelings, conflict, pain, fear, shame – never ends well. When you purposefully avoid something, you are shoving it deeper inside. You're creating negativity inside your mind and body. Negativity will literally tear apart your mental and physical health.

While growing up, I was completely aware that my parents didn't have a lot of resources. As I got older and performed well in my career, I started making a decent salary and had a positive net worth. I was excited about this progress. I no longer consciously thought about being broke.

One day I was shopping with a friend. I had picked up a couple items to purchase. At the checkout I decided I really didn't need these items. My friend jokingly called me *poor*. Emotions instantly came to the surface. I realized that deep-down I still felt poor even though financially I wasn't poor any longer. I had no idea these feelings were still inside of me. I was happy she made that joke because it revealed some of my shame.

You may not have a friend reveal this to you, so take the time to analyze yourself. Figure out what is lying just below the surface of your conscious mind. It's only when you discover what is holding you back that you can release it and move forward.

Instead of practicing avoidance or ignorance, face it head-on. Whatever you are pushing down, let it come to the surface and face it. You will never move ahead if you don't. You will feel stuck like you do right now until you acknowledge it.

Feeling stuck in your circumstances, your environment, or your progress is a horrible feeling. I know because I've been there. I've felt stuck in my past. These feelings will not go away on their own. You've got to be courageous and face whatever you're avoiding. Recognize your feelings. Acknowledge why you feel this way.

When I was spending like crazy, I was in denial. I wasn't aware of how big my debt pile had become. Instead of wanting to know, it seemed easier to live in the dark. I had tricked myself into believing everything was fine. I thought, *eventually, I'll get a promotion and out earn my growing debt.* I wasn't taking it seriously. I was just burying my concerns. This attitude of ignorance and avoidance wasn't allowing me to progress. I was stuck.

After a few years of this, I slowly got more serious about my desire to get out of debt. I started seeing hope.

When you're in a hole so big it doesn't look like there is any way out, it's difficult to believe that escaping is possible. Instead of trying to find hope, we immediately brush off the idea.

However, when you see a tiny ray of hope, that small amount of light might be all you need to get started.

No matter how much debt you've accumulated, it's time to start believing you can do anything you set your mind to. It's time to start facing your fears. This might include opening your statements, having that hard conversation, or listing your debts.

The negative emotion that is stopping you from taking this action is the reason you are stuck. When we feel less confident, we are likely to spend more. We feel a need to compensate externally when we feel insecure internally.

I'm going to ask you to take some difficult actions in this book. You'll need to confront your fears, shame, guilt, whatever is holding you back.

I know ignorance and avoidance isn't your path.

Myth 1: Money is Just Math

Money isn't just math.

Today, we not only have cash, but we have a massive industry built upon credit. We can borrow funds to buy just about anything we want. There are an endless number of ways to get money immediately instead of waiting for that next paycheck. These options have created complexity in our emotions with money. Credit has completely skewed our perception of how much money we really have.

With credit we can live the same amazing lifestyle as those around us, even if we don't have as much income or wealth. We can buy the same products, drive the same cars, and own similar houses. This is what credit has allowed us to do. We can use it to create a *fabulous* lifestyle, even though we can barely afford the monthly payments.

We have built expectations in our heads of the lifestyle we *deserve*. Our friends all have a house in a certain area, so we should too. Our friends have the newest phone, so we should too. Our egos are strong forces. We want to keep up a certain image or reputation, plus we work really hard, so why shouldn't we have everything we want? The world has been created for the consumer, right? Companies offer creative financing therefore we can *afford* that new item today.

With the inception of credit, a dollar in your pocket does not mean you only have a dollar to spend. If you have a credit card, you may have $1,000 to spend.

And, once you've charged that $1,000 on the card, now you owe interest on that balance.

You see your friends driving a new car, and you decide you want a new car. They either paid cash or borrowed on a three-year loan term. However, you can't afford the monthly payments on a three-year loan, so you decide to go for the 84-month or 96-month term. That's seven-to-eight years you will be paying for this car. Think about that. Do you really want a vehicle that you will be paying for over the next eight years? That would be like making payments on your 2015 vehicle right now in 2023. Just because we have access to credit doesn't mean we need to use it. Living a lifestyle or keeping up an image you can't afford isn't something you can manage in the long term, and it doesn't really make you happy.

This is why money isn't just math. We are emotional beings. We have proud egos, expectations of what we think we deserve, and our image to uphold. All these intangibles cost money to keep up – money we don't have. Humble your ego, give up your expectations, and be happy with what you have. When you accept these, money will become math again.

The Real Source of Happiness

Does it really make us happy to buy new things even when we don't have the cash to pay for them?

In the moment, yes, we get a release of dopamine, a hormone that produces a feeling of pleasure, but that dopamine high is only temporary. It fades fast. Our brains get used to the familiar very quickly, which means the new car you purchased last month is already familiar.

It's not new. It doesn't give you the same excitement it did when you first bought it. Dopamine feelings from new purchases are temporary. This isn't real happiness.

I remember during a summer in between college years, I was living with my parents and working in a factory as labor. This particular summer, I was working third shift, from 11pm to 7am every night. I got into a routine where my mom and I would go to the local gym every morning after work. I would then go home and sleep most of the day away, getting up a couple hours before going to work the next night.

Working nights was not for me. I wasn't seeing my friends, and when I did, I was tired. I wasn't happy this summer like I had been in past summers. My mom and I went shopping at one point, and I told her I just needed to buy something to feel happy. I wish I had known then what I know now. True happiness doesn't come from buying things. It might have felt good in the moment, but the wallet I purchased didn't really make me happy. If I had taken some time to really understand the cause of my unhappiness, I would have been able to overcome it much easier. The real cause was the uncertainty in my life. I didn't know what I wanted to do, and I was taking on student loans that I didn't know how I would pay back. The growing debt and uncertainty were the real reasons behind my unhappiness, and the hours I was working didn't help either.

True happiness comes from the inside, not from external purchases. Don't let your fascination with external influences and the latest trends be your source of happiness. You will be very disappointed. Instead of wasting your money on stuff that doesn't matter, start appreciating all the little things you have already.

Action 1 – Practice Gratitude

True happiness is felt when you genuinely tune-in to gratitude. Your action is to write down three things you're thankful for each day. Don't go and buy a fancy notebook. I have a simple notebook that I bought for $1. Be very specific and try not to repeat items every day.

For example, 1. I got to play basketball with my family. 2. My dog made me laugh during our walk yesterday, and 3. We finished tiling the backsplash over the weekend.

The more detailed moments you can recollect, the more powerful gratitude is. Relive those experiences from the day before and let yourself smile or laugh. If you're just happy you got a good night's sleep, then think about how nice it is to have a warm, comfortable bed. You can be thankful for people, experiences, or things. This exercise is very personal, and there are no wrong answers.

Consistently practicing gratitude everyday creates more positivity in your life. Replaying these positive events in your mind creates more positive thoughts as you are reliving the positive experience when you write them down.

We naturally think in pictures. When you write down what you're thankful for, it takes effort to convert the pictures in your head into words on paper. This extra effort has a stronger impact on your mind.

The amazing thing about gratitude is when you think about those moments, you can't be worried at the same time. Try this and prove me wrong. Take a minute to concentrate on all the small things you have in your life. Genuinely be thankful for them.

Were you able to worry at the same time, or were thoughts of gratitude dominating your mind?

Gratitude Can Save You Money

Look around at all you have. Do you have a place to call home? Did you have something to eat today and access to water? You most likely take all of this for granted, but these are the simple things in life we need to recognize and appreciate. Not everyone has these simple things. Maybe you don't have the nicest house, but it keeps you dry and warm. Start appreciating everything you have, even if it isn't the shiniest or the best, it's yours. I started practicing gratitude a few years ago and wow, what a difference. I see more of the goodness in my life everyday – from the silly moments with the pets to how good exercising makes me feel. There are so many good moments in our lives, and if you're not paying attention, you will miss them.

Once you start making gratitude a priority in your life, you will start noticing things you've never noticed before. I live in a rural area not too far from a river. I was at my desk working one day and happened to look out the window at exactly the right moment. There was an eagle flying over the cornfield. It was the coolest sight. It's easy to overlook the beauty in this world if we're not living with gratitude in our minds. Open your eyes and see the goodness in this world.

Gratitude, appreciation, and recognition for everything you already have opens your eyes and shows you what's most important in life. You realize you don't need to spend as much to be happy. That extra pair of jeans isn't going to give you true joy.

When you figure out gratitude, you are ready to get out of debt. Eliminating your debt isn't just about sacrifice, it's about appreciating what's in your life already and prioritizing it appropriately.

It's time to tune into the happiness channel by being grateful. External items and influences won't truly make you happy; they only cause temporary excitement, and those feelings fade fast. The sooner you understand this, the faster you can start your millionaire journey.

Turning Point #1

Your mindset is the hurdle standing in the way of you taking control over your money. Instead of seeing money as the tool to buy things, see it as the tool to get wealthy. We all know this intrinsically, but many of us equate more money with more stuff. Do you ever think, *when I get my bonus from work, I'm going on a shopping spree or I'm upgrading my car*? I used to think this way. I would get excited about more money because that meant more stuff.

What finally changed my behavior was a television clip I saw of Suze Orman. She was talking to a woman who was having issues limiting her spending. Suze brought out a rack of clothes from this woman's closet worth $6500 and a pile of cash worth $6500. She asked her, *'would you rather have these clothes or this handful of cash?'*

For me, this question was so powerful. I finally realized I would rather have the cash than the clothes. Cash is security. Cash allows me to retire comfortably. Sacrificing some of the extras, like clothes, today doesn't hurt me, but not having cash really hurts my future.

I don't know why I didn't see this sooner. A lightbulb finally went off.

Why was I frivolously spending on consumption of these non-valuable, depreciating things when I could be investing that money or paying down my debt?

Spent Money is Lost Time

You work hard for your money. Why do you work hard? You desire a certain lifestyle, and that lifestyle costs money. It's very cyclical. The more we want to buy, the more we need to earn. However, the more we earn, the more we buy. Many of us get caught up in this vicious cycle without really being aware we are in it.

Instead of succumbing to this cycle, start thinking of your spending in terms of how many hours of work are required to purchase that item. Let's say you want a new pair of shoes that costs $75. If you make $15 per hour, that's five hours of work just for that one pair of shoes. If you make $25 per hour, that's three hours of your time and effort for that pair of shoes. How long have you wanted those shoes? Have you been saving up or is this an impulse buy? How many pairs of similar shoes do you already have?

How many hours of your life are you willing to give up to buy that next thing? What if you delayed a big purchase, like a vehicle? Would it be worth it to retire a few years earlier, but drive your cars longer?

A friend of mine who is very frugal was the CFO (Chief Financial Officer) for a manufacturing site. This was a prominent role. She was very good at this job and didn't let the peer pressure of keeping up appearances get to her. She drove a 20-year-old Honda that was beat up to say the least. One evening the car didn't start. Someone on her team figured out how to start it for her. The passenger door handle didn't work and had to be opened with a screw that was strategically placed. Driving this car never really bothered her. She did eventually get embarrassed when her boss, the global CFO came to town from London and needed a ride. She admitted at that point it was time to get a new car. This friend is financially free today. She doesn't have to work. Because she made choices like this, she is free to live the rest of her life exactly how she wants to live it.

As you go shopping, start asking yourself if those items are worth that many additional hours of work.

You may not think each dollar is important, but you must start with this fundamental belief that every dollar is, in fact, important. It's only when you can manage the few dollars that you will be given more to manage. If you can't manage a little money, do you think you could manage a lot of money? Probably not. You would likely fall prey to the same spending behaviors you have today and before you know it, that windfall would be gone.

2: Perspective is Underrated

Our thoughts and beliefs, which create our perspective, not only have the power to change how we see the world, but also change our world.

When my perspective finally changed, my behavior followed. I needed that question from Suze Orman, *would you rather have this rack of clothes or this pile of cash?* This is what finally made me see that clothes can't provide security in the future. Clothes and other depreciating items won't help me retire early. They won't help me reach my goals. They are just things. They don't really matter. They will likely be in the garbage or donation pile in a few years. Cash, on the other hand, is a tool. Cash does give me security. Cash can help me retire early. I can use cash to create more cash by buying appreciating assets. Cash can be used in so many ways and will retain its value more than things.

My old perspective was so skewed. I used to think, *if I pay off all my debt, then I won't have anything to motivate me to keep working hard.* I thought the monthly payments on my car and other toys were the source of my motivation. The monthly payments were a motivator to keep working hard, but I had this completely wrong. Why would someone want to work her whole life just to be in debt her whole life? My mindset has completely changed from that old mentality. I no longer have debt and am more motivated than ever before. When numbers are positive, opportunities arise, stress alleviates, and creativity flows.

Another misconception I believed was if I made more money, then I could have more stuff. I wish the alarm bells would have gone off then. It's true, if you make more, you can have more, but you shouldn't keep spending everything you make. This strategy will never let you become truly wealthy. Think about someone making $100,000 salary and spending $95,000 every year, and then think about someone making $60,000 salary and only spending $30,000 every year. The second person is much better off. She is investing $30,000 per year while the first person is only investing $5,000. Increasing your lifestyle every time you get a raise isn't going to allow you to retire early or to become wealthy. Instead, you'll just end up with a lot of stuff.

Myth 2: You Can Afford It If Your Monthly Income is Greater than Your Monthly Payments

<u>**Adopt a long-term mindset, not a short-term mindset.**</u>

When you consider getting a new car or a new toy, do you think about the total loan value, or is your decision based solely on the monthly payment? A couple of my friends do this. They trade in their vehicles every three to four years. They always explain what a good deal they got because they have a new vehicle, and the monthly payment is the same or lower than the old car's payment. To them, it's all about the monthly payment amount. They don't consider the length of time they'll be paying on this loan or the interest rate they are paying. They never mention the total loan value. They expect to have a car payment for the rest of their lives.

When you make decisions based on only your monthly payments, it's like you're in the middle of an unfamiliar forest. You're hiking without a map. All you see are a lot of trees. You can see a few steps ahead of you, but the path isn't clear.

If you want to get out of debt and accumulate wealth, it's time to change your perspective. Look at your total debt balances instead of your monthly payments.

When you look at your total debt balances, you're adopting the long-term view. You're flying over the forest, where you can clearly see the path. It's only when you see your total debt that you realize how much you need to pay off.

We have normalized debt in today's society to the point where many of us expect to have debt our entire lives. In high school I remember thinking my parents were so strange because they never took on debt. They paid their house off in 15 years and spent very little each month. As a teenager I wasn't a fan. They didn't make much money and living off what they made was difficult. It meant we didn't get many extras. I look back now and think, *wow, my parents did that correctly. They didn't succumb to the pressure of debt.*

If you are living with a month-to-month mindset, one emergency can throw you completely off. Many unplanned things come up, from a new medical bill to a flat tire to the unnecessary impulse buy. These unexpected costs can lead to additional credit card charges, growing debt balances, and increased interest expenses.

You may think you are young and have plenty of time to catch up on your retirement savings later, but the problem is that as time goes by, you lose more opportunities to invest.

In your twenties, you are in the beginning of your career; your income can only go up from here, right? You'll have time to make the necessary cutbacks later. However, as time goes by, your attitude doesn't change. Instead of holding onto that car longer, you see a brand new one that you feel you need. You've been promoted at work and need to look the part. Your mindset doesn't change like you thought it would. You've actually grown more stubborn in your ways and are less likely to change as you've aged.

Now, you're in your forties and you still feel you have plenty of time to catch up. Again, your mindset hasn't changed. The issue is that you've lost a lot of years to invest because you have been living with the month-to-month perspective. Until you see the whole picture – your entire debt balances – you will not truly understand what type of hole you're in.

I want you to start imagining your life without debt. I know this can feel unrealistic. You may have very little hope that you can dig yourself out of the mess you've made. Believe me; I've been there. I didn't know if I could really figure it out. I knew I had to try though, and you must too.

Your Attitude Makes or Breaks You

Like I mentioned earlier, mindset is a combination of your attitude, beliefs, thoughts, and outlook. Your mindset is your understanding of the world around you. It determines whether you achieve your goals, or you quit early. It determines whether you even try to achieve a goal or not.

Your deep-rooted beliefs influence your mindset significantly. If you've grown up with people around you who play the victim role, then you may gravitate toward playing a victim as well. If you grew up with people who pushed through barriers, then you will likely see challenges as growth opportunities.

Your mindset is why you picked up this book to read. You know you are capable of becoming wealthy. You know deep down you can do this. Your mindset is in the right spot. You're ready to start this journey. You know it's not going to be easy, but that doesn't matter. It's going to be worth it.

Your attitude plays a huge role in your mindset. It doesn't just play a role within your debt-to-millionaire journey; it plays a huge role in your life. I always knew my attitude was important, but never realized how important it was until a few years ago. We were doing the annual roundtable at my company where the managers and director meet and discuss the individuals on their teams to give them their annual performance ratings. Each manager says a few words about his or her team members and then the other managers chip in with their experiences of that person. There was a team member who got her job done. She was very competent. I had a decent relationship with her, but I discovered no one else had that. She butted heads with everyone else. She was negative. She made it clear that she wasn't happy in finance.

Even though she did a good job when it came to her actual tasks, her attitude was so bad that she received a lower rating. To put this in context, there were about 20 team members in total, and usually only two received the lower ratings. This team member who did her job fine received one of the lowest ratings of all 20 people because her attitude was bad. For me, this was a total surprise. I knew attitude was important, but never realized just how important it was.

Whatever path you take, make sure you've got the right attitude going into it. Your attitude makes or breaks you.

Scarcity versus Abundance Mindset

There are two mindsets when it comes to having enough: scarcity and abundance. Those with the scarcity mindset think our resources are limited. There is only so much to go around, and they will never have enough. They think the pie is the total. If someone else gets a bigger piece, then there will be less available to everyone else. They also believe they will never be good enough, they will never have enough, they aren't smart enough, they don't look good enough, and they never have enough time.

Zig Ziglar said, "lack of direction, not lack of time, is the problem. We all have twenty-four-hour days."

When I first heard this quote, it hit me. We all have the same amount of time each day. It's up to us to choose how we spend it. Are we focused on our goals, or do we let time fly by without intentionality? Do we jump from idea to idea sporadically, or do we decide to go in one direction persistently?

As you can imagine, scarcity thinking drives negativity and limiting thoughts. People who have this mindset feel no hope of change. They are so deeply rooted in their limits they don't even try to improve their conditions. They believe their current circumstances are permanent.

Comparison increases scarcity thinking. If your friends buy new cars, and you are driving an old clunker, you might allow thoughts of unworthiness to enter your mind. Your car doesn't define who you are though. Your friends might have taken out loans on those cars while you are debt free. Who's in the better financial position? You have peace of mind. You are not defined by the things you possess.

The opposite of the scarcity mindset is the abundance mindset. The abundance thinkers know there is enough for everyone. When they see their brother's income increase dramatically, they don't think, 'shoot, he got a bigger piece of the pie.' Instead, they think, 'awesome for him. If he can do it, I can do it.'

The number of resources isn't limited. It's not reduced to a pie-shape with everyone getting a percentage. Have you seen the trends in gross domestic product (GDP)? Gross domestic product is a statistic that represents the total value of goods and services produced in a country each year. If you search in Google, "US GDP chart", you'll find a bunch of websites that show a chart with an increasing trendline. This country and many others produce more and more every single year. There isn't a limit to the wealth that can be created. It's not a pie-shaped limit; it's infinity. If your friends find ways to earn more money, it doesn't make your ability to earn more money harder. Your friends' higher income could very well lead to your higher income.

The abundance mindset is the only way to live. It's the only way you can achieve your goals. Be happy when your brother and friends earn more. That means you can earn more too. Stop wasting your time believing you aren't good enough. Every single person on this planet contributes a different skill set and brings new ideas. The fact that you are alive is an achievement in itself. Know that you are enough. You might need to develop skills to earn the income you want to earn, but that doesn't mean you're less than; it only means you need training and education.

One thing that amazes me is the number of success stories that started in garages. Jeff Bezos started Amazon in his garage. We all see that giant company today and think he never had any struggles. Look at all he has. The fact is he didn't always have what he has today. He didn't even have a separate location when he started. Amazon was just an idea in the beginning. He persevered through the challenges, through the struggles, and through all the naysayers. He saw the vision. He understood the abundance mindset.

Know that whoever you look up to today was once where you are. They started at the beginning, changing their beliefs, eliminating their negativity, and expanding their minds.

You only have time for so many thoughts in your conscious mind each day. Maximize these thoughts by focusing on the positive and believing in abundance.

Build Your Inner Confidence

I read the book, *Think and Grow Rich*, by Napoleon Hill a few years ago, and it completely changed my life. We can do anything we want to do. We just need to have confidence and belief in ourselves. What a difference this book has made. I've taken actions these past few years that I didn't have the confidence to take prior to this. One example is public speaking. I've always hated it. I didn't want the attention. I didn't like my voice. I could go on and on why I didn't want to get up in front of anyone and speak. However, last year I joined Toastmasters. I've given many speeches and already see a huge difference in my public speaking ability.

My self-confidence used to fluctuate based on external circumstances. When I moved from Los Angeles back to Ohio, I was on top of the world. I had just graduated with my MBA and wasn't bothered that I didn't have a job when I moved. I knew I would find a great position. I had complete confidence at that time. Then, a few years later, I applied for a job in my company that I didn't get, and my confidence was shattered. I almost left the company over it.

It's very easy to let your surrounding circumstances dictate your confidence, but that's not the right way to go about it. You are who you are and bring the same value in any situation. Grow your confidence from the inside out and don't let external influences dictate how confident you are.

Amy Cuddy gave an amazing TED talk on how our posture impacts our confidence. This is her advice from the speech. Stand up straight, shoulders back, and arms open. Widen your stance. The more open you stand, the more confident you will feel. When people cower into themselves, crossing their arms, wilting their shoulders, their confidence level goes down. Hormones change in your body based on your posture. Try this exercise. Even if you just do it for one minute, it works. You will feel it.

Deciding to get control of your money is a life-changing decision. With this one decision, you are literally changing the trajectory of your life. How you feel on the inside is reflected outwardly. It's time to break through your money fears and move into action.

Make Choices for Your Future Self

Every day you make choices. Do your choices help you today or help you in the future? If you start making choices for your future self, your life is going to change in big ways.

This can be difficult though. As human beings, it's much easier to make choices for ourselves right now and for things we can see. If you want a soda and candy bar right now, and you have access to the soda and candy bar, then it's going to be tough to stop yourself from enjoying these. They are right at your fingertips. You can see them. You can touch them. They are tangible.

This makes saving for that illusive retirement difficult. You can't see it. You can't touch it. It's so far in the future. When we can't see something with our own eyes, it makes it very hard to believe. It makes it even more difficult to change our behavior today for our future self.

Has anyone ever tried to convince you to change your beliefs, but they can't prove their belief is truer than yours? If they can't show you tangible proof, then why would you believe them? Why would you change your behavior? It's very similar here. You see your current self today and want to optimize your life today. You are here now. You can't look in the mirror and see your future self. You can't open your eyes and see your future retirement. This makes money difficult. We live in the present. We want to maximize our present life and have an awesome retirement. However, the caveat is we need to sacrifice some spending in one of our lives – our present life or our retirement life.

People living with the month-to-month mindset are choosing to sacrifice their retirement. They are choosing their present over their future. To become wealthy, you've got to flip your priorities. You've got to choose your future self over your present self.

I always try to keep my future self the priority. It helps in decision-making, especially when it comes to money. Do I want to purchase an item today or would having that extra money in my account tomorrow feel better? If you start thinking this way, you will make different decisions. Think about your future self in five years or even next year. What can you do today to give your future self a better life? Do you want extra money in your account, or do you want to buy a toy that you'll use five times a year? If you get that extra errand done after work tonight, does that give you more time tomorrow night to spend with your kids?

Life is all about choices and trade-offs. What we consume today won't be there tomorrow.

Start taking the road less traveled and invest in your future self, whether that be financially through retirement investing, intellectually through learning a new skill, or physically by improving your diet and exercise. All these investments might be harder today, but they will pay off incredibly in the long run.

If you don't start now, in a year are you going to look back and wish you had started today?

Create a Vision

I have a friend who got into trouble in high school. She was hanging out with the wrong crowd and drinking and smoking the wrong things. She was naturally a rebel, not wanting to listen to authority. It got so bad she had to take summer classes to graduate. And then, with her low GPA she couldn't get into any of the colleges she wanted, so she went to a local junior college for a couple semesters to prove she could excel. After this, she was accepted into a great university and graduated with the rest of her class. She found a job in her field and went to work. She not only worked, but also went to school at night to get her MBA. She is now financially independent.

What turned her around? What took her from the rebellious high school student barely graduating to a financially independent adult? As she rebelled, she was aware of how those around her lived. She was aware that if she continued acting this way, this would be her future. This awareness was her turning point. This awareness established what she didn't want her future to look like and allowed her to create a vision of what she wanted her future to look like. As this vision became clearer, her desire to change became stronger.

Take a few minutes to think about your vision. What is it you want your life to look like in 10, 20, or 30 years? If you were 80 years old, what is your ideal life? Is there something you wish you would have done?

I've always wanted to retire early. The age I retire fluctuates though. I can't pinpoint the year it will happen, but I know it's going to happen in the next decade. This doesn't mean I will stop working altogether. I have two main pursuits I want to accomplish after I've officially retired from my corporate job. My vision keeps me inspired.

Financial freedom is likely in everyone's vision. It's natural to want to be free from having to do anything, free from working for a company, and free to spend your time exactly how you want. Financial freedom is possible for everyone. You may be thinking, *no way this doesn't happen in my world*, but I'm telling you it's possible. It takes action, effort, and work. I'm not saying it's going to be easy, because it won't be easy. However, it will be worth it.

When you have a vision of what you want, you're more willing to wake up like my friend did and turn your life around. That vision comes with awareness. Meditation is a great tool for awareness.

Action 2 – Start Meditating

Meditation is a great way to get outside of your thoughts. If you've never meditated, this might seem strange. How do you get outside your thoughts? Meditation teaches you to separate yourself from your thoughts. There are different analogies, such as think of your mind as the sky and your thoughts as the clouds. You can let them float by without reacting to them or you can engage with them. Another analogy is to think of your mind as the highway and your thoughts as the cars. You don't have to get inside the cars. You can just observe them speeding by.

Both analogies are powerful. They demonstrate our power to separate ourselves from our thoughts. We don't have to be controlled by our thoughts or our emotions. We can rise above them.

When you have the power to observe your thoughts, you gain the power to question your thoughts, beliefs, and emotions. Everything you believed in the past might not be the truth. Having the ability to question those deep-rooted beliefs opens your mind to many possibilities.

I've always wanted to retire early. I thought if I worked hard for 20 years I could retire early – put in more hours at the beginning and have freedom for the rest of my life. I had heard about meditation years ago, but I thought this was for later, when I had more time. I was of the mindset that I needed to work hard and accumulate a lot of money first. Then I would have time for meditation later.

That's when I needed meditation the most. That's when I needed to control my stress levels. That's when I needed to calm my mind.

Make yourself a promise to fit it in. Start small. Set aside five minutes a day to begin with. Take a deep breath – 4 seconds in and 4 seconds out. That's all it takes to start.

As you breathe slower and deeper, inhaling through your nose, more oxygen is being taken into your body and your brain. It is circulating much more widely than when you take short, shallow breaths. This act of deep breathing feels relaxing and calming.

When you take deep, slow breaths, and hold them, you are actually resetting your nervous system. This is why it feels so good. Taking a deep, slow breath literally reduces the feeling of stress immediately. If you try this, feel the calmness that emits. Feel how your state of awareness changes.

To optimize this, combine your gratitude with your deep breathing.

3: Figure Out Your Destination

When you want to go somewhere you've never been before, how do you get there?

You could ask a friend who's already been there, or you could use a GPS. For your GPS to work correctly, you must have an ending destination. The GPS can't guide you where you want to go without it. Similarly, we will drive through life in circles if we don't have a destination in mind.

If you don't know what you want, then how will you get it? The simple answer is you won't. You'll continue running in a rat race you can never win.

When I was fully committed to getting out of debt, I had hope, I had commitment, and I had a great desire. I could visualize those balances going down and being paid off. My destination was to be debt-free. I focused on that destination and created a plan to get there.

For any goal, you've got to get specific. You must know exactly what you want and why you want it. The end goal must be so specific that you can visualize it. If you can't visualize it, then it's not specific enough.

In this case, your goal might be to be debt free, to be financially free, or to become a millionaire. Whatever your goal is, get specific. If it's to be debt free, figure out what your deadline is and how much needs to be paid off. If your goal is to be financially free, define what financial freedom means to you. Does it mean a certain amount of money in the bank, or does it mean a minimum amount of monthly passive income?

Myth 3: Your Goals Should be Easily Achievable

<u>**Stretch yourself with your goals.**</u>

If you know you can achieve something, where's the challenge? What's the point of the goal? For example, if your salary is $50,000 a year, and your company gives a 2% annual merit increase, then your goal to earn $51,000 next year isn't much of a stretch. You basically need to maintain your job performance, and you'll end up with the 2% raise at $51,000. That doesn't seem very exciting.

When your goals are easily achievable, you aren't stretching yourself. You're sticking to your comfort zone. You're assuming that what you think you can't do, you won't be able to do.

If you don't believe you can get out of debt, then you would never attempt it. If becoming financially free sounds impossible, you would never create that goal. What a boring existence if we never created goals that we thought weren't achievable. You've got to think bigger.

I give myself stretch goals all the time. Six years ago, I was looking at my personal finances at the end of the year and gave myself the goal to make an extra $10,000 in the new year. I had no idea how I was going to do this, but I thought it would be a fun challenge.

I had a few ideas throughout the year and tried a couple attempts, but I didn't achieve it in that first year. I made a few hundred extra dollars. That was it.

Instead of giving up, I flipped a property in the following year and made an extra $31,000. Then, the year after that, I flipped another property and gained an extra $23,000. In the year that followed, I switched my attention from flipping real estate to stocks. I traded some stocks and made even more. I could have easily given up after that first year of not achieving my goal, but I didn't. I stuck with it, trying to figure out the puzzle.

You don't have to know the 'how' when you write out your goal. You only need to know your destination. The 'how' will come to you in time as you continue to be committed, persistent, and patient.

Make it fun. Don't create unnecessary stress over this goal. Create a game out of it.

When you give yourself stretch goals, you will achieve more. You will grow more. You may not accomplish every goal you create, but you will gain so much more in personal growth. I have failed to achieve goals more times than I can count, but I'm still here. It's okay to fail, as long as you keep trying.

Limitations are Self-Fulfilling

During the onboarding at my first job out of college, I was in training with a new branch manager. We both had to understand the job of Teller for our roles, so our trainer took us through different transactions. My colleague used big numbers for all her transactions, while I used $50, $100, and $500 for mine. She said, "you've got to think big." I never really considered the truth in her statement. I've always steadily progressed through my career, getting raises every now and then, but didn't realize how powerful her thoughts and the use of large numbers was. It's so true and I understand its power today. If you had told me as a college student what my salary was going to be at age 42, I never would have believed you. It took years of growing and progressively thinking bigger and bigger to get to where I am today.

The more personal limits you break, the more easily it is to see that bigger is doable. I remember being at that same job at the bank, making a salary of $22,500 barely able to make my student loan payments, and handing a $100,000 check to a woman after she sold a property. I thought this was awesome. She didn't have a mortgage, and she literally had $100,000 in her hand. I pondered how I could be in that position someday. It took a little over a decade, but I got to accept my first check for over $100,000 that partially belonged to me when I sold my second flip property. There are moments like this in my life, where I can still visualize being in that original bank conference room handing that customer her check. It makes me think about the crazy, amazing journey that life is when you keep learning and pushing yourself.

Never believe your current situation is permanent. I could have settled for a local job and never reached past my childhood environment, but I knew there were other opportunities out there. I knew I didn't have to settle. You don't either. Your current situation is just a step toward your future. Don't put limits in your mind when they don't really exist. Too many of us create these invisible limits in our careers, in our relationships, in our salaries, and in our finances. Once we hit what we think are our limits, we stop trying. We stop pursuing better. We stop pursuing more. We settle for enough. These limits aren't real though; you've just made assumptions in your mind. Remove these limits from your mind. You can do anything you put your mind to.

Getting out of debt is hard, especially in the beginning. You've become accustomed to spending without consideration of the financial consequences. You've created a comfortable lifestyle, and cutting some of that is going to be difficult. It wasn't easy for me to stop unnecessary spending. It wasn't easy for me to start tracking my debts and expenses. This isn't going to be easy. You may not see the light at the end of the tunnel for the first few months. Stick to your plan though. This is a long-term behavior change. Imagine seeing your debt eliminated and your net worth exceeding a million dollars. It's going to be worth it.

Burning Desire

How bad do you want to get out of debt? How bad do you want to become a millionaire?

You've got to really want it. The more you think about your goal and the more emotion you have toward your goal, the quicker you will come up with the answers to achieve it.

Napoleon Hill called this a burning desire in his book, *Think and Grow Rich*. You've got to have not only a desire to get out of debt or become financially free, but you've got to have a burning desire.

A few years ago, I decided I wanted to be a real estate agent, something I had thought about for many years prior. I was flipping houses part-time, and this was a huge benefit as we had the flexibility to look at houses at our convenience and save money on commissions. Part of the onboarding training of the real estate company I joined asked us to write down our short-term and long-term goals as well as fill out a schedule, writing in how we would spend our time each day of the week. I was already working a full-time job, so on the schedule I put that I would start waking up at 5am each morning to do property research, memorize scripts, and look for potential clients from 5-7am before my other job started. Then, I would have a few hours in the evening for working out and doing a little more real estate before bed.

The problem was my desire wasn't burning that hot. I didn't have the feelings or emotions I should have had. I couldn't get myself out of bed at 5am. I tried multiple days and weeks to set the alarm at 5am, but I kept hitting the snooze button. I realized the desire to sell real estate for extra money wasn't there for me.

What would you sacrifice to achieve this desire? Many professional athletes live in the gym or on the course or in the pool. They are obsessed with their sport. They sacrifice seeing their families and friends for holidays in order to travel with their teams. They wouldn't be professionals if they didn't sacrifice a part of themselves in order to give more to their sport.

Sue Bird is a well-known basketball player who played for UConn and for the WNBA team, Seattle Storm, for almost two decades. She grew up playing sports. She transferred high schools to be part of a better program. She has broken many records throughout high school, college, and her professional career. She, like many other professional players, spent many seasons abroad, in Europe and Russia, sacrificing time with her family and friends. The sacrifice is tremendous, but the rewards are tremendous as well. She has stayed on her journey even when things got tough, because that was her burning desire.

When you are absolutely certain about your desire, the hard times only make you stronger. When you know what your goal is, nothing will stop you from attaining it.

If the goal of getting out of debt doesn't feel that important to you, what about the goal of financial freedom which gives you complete control over your time? Being financially free means your money is invested in assets which return enough money for you to live on, meaning you no longer need to work. You can live on your passive income instead. If that doesn't motivate you, I'm not sure what will.

Beanstalk Goals

When we use systems – processes, tools, and habits – to achieve our goals, we get much more accomplished in less time. Think about your job. There are processes and tools in place to promote more efficient and effective working. The most tangible example is an assembly line. This is a system where widgets are produced more quickly than if the same group of people working on the assembly line got together and tried to produce them without any systems, tools, or organization. When you have a system in place, you work more effectively. You get more done.

I love creating systems in my job and in my personal life to work better, faster, and more effectively, therefore I came up with my own goal system called, *Beanstalk Goals*. *Beanstalk Goals* helps to illustrate how goals are achieved and provides a common structure for all our goals. As the name sounds, the structure is a beanstalk.

Remember the story of Jack and the Beanstalk? Jack and his mom didn't have much money. He took a risk and purchased seeds, which did not please his mom. To their surprise, the seeds grew into a giant beanstalk. He climbed to the top of the beanstalk and ran into a monster that wanted to eat him. Jack decided to keep going when the monster awoke instead of escaping back down the beanstalk. Because he didn't give up, he saved a hen and a harp before leaving. To his surprise, the hen produced golden eggs, giving Jack and his mom much more income.

Similar to Jack's adventure, your ultimate goal sits at the top of the beanstalk. Your ultimate goal is a BIG goal, a longer-term goal, something that seems out of reach. The objective is to get to the top of your beanstalk. There will be many obstacles, failures, and setbacks to get there though, just like Jack faced when he ran into the monster.

At the top of your beanstalk, write down specifically what your goal is and why you want it.

The what and the why are both very important. If you think you know what you want to achieve, but don't know why you want to achieve it, this journey is going to be more difficult. For example, if your house is on fire, and inside was a family album you wanted, would you go in after it? Now, what if one of your children or parents were inside that house? Would you go in and get them? The why on the second scenario is much more important than an album. You likely wouldn't risk your life for an album, but for a helpless family member, you most likely would. Your why is the key to how much you will risk and how hard you will work to achieve your goal. The more important your why is to you, the more likely you will achieve your goal.

The top represents a stretch goal, a BIG goal. No one is going to achieve this in a day, week, or month. Next, you'll break this BIG goal down into smaller goals.

You can apply this Beanstalk Goals method to any goal, but since this book is specifically how to improve your money, let's look at the goal of paying off your debt. The only improvement I would make to this top goal in the below example is to state exactly how much debt needs to be paid off.

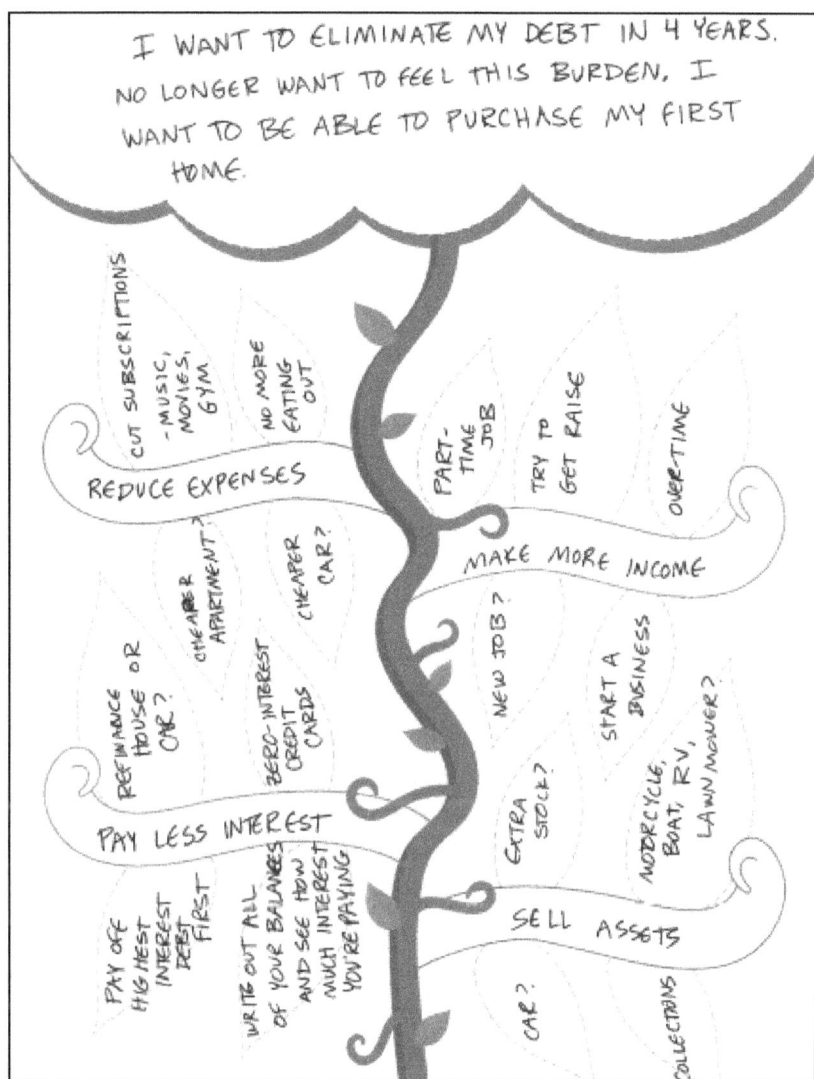

I WANT TO ELIMINATE MY DEBT IN 4 YEARS. NO LONGER WANT TO FEEL THIS BURDEN. I WANT TO BE ABLE TO PURCHASE MY FIRST HOME.

REDUCE EXPENSES
- CUT SUBSCRIPTIONS - MUSIC, MOVIES, GYM
- NO MORE EATING OUT

MAKE MORE INCOME
- PART-TIME JOB
- TRY TO GET RAISE
- OVER-TIME

PAY LESS INTEREST
- CHEAPER APARTMENT?
- CHEAPER CAR?
- REFINANCE HOUSE OR CAR?
- ZERO-INTEREST CREDIT CARDS
- PAY OFF HIGHEST INTEREST DEBT FIRST
- WRITE OUT ALL OF YOUR BALANCES AND SEE HOW MUCH INTEREST YOU'RE PAYING

MAKE MORE INCOME
- NEW JOB?
- START A BUSINESS
- EXTRA STOCK?
- MOTORCYCLE, BOAT, RV, LAWN MOWER?

SELL ASSETS
- CAR?
- COLLECTIONS

The vines that grow off the beanstalk represent the smaller, shorter-term goals. What smaller things can you do in the next few months to build momentum toward your big goals?

In this example they are: 1. Reduce expenses, 2. Make more income, 3. Pay less interest, and 4. Sell assets. These were some ideas that kickstarted my debt-free journey. I'm sure there are many others you can come up with.

You'll notice there are multiple vines and many leaves. Most long-term goals are so big that there are multiple paths and multiple things you can do to achieve them. This beanstalk illustration is meant to be a structure for brainstorming, not necessarily a list of everything you need to do. Writing down all your ideas puts them on paper and allows you to choose later which actions you want to take.

The ideas on the vines are still pretty big goals and aren't very specific. For example, how does this person intend to reduce expenses?

This is what the leaves are for – the very specific, actionable goals that can be achieved today or this week. In this example, under 1. Reduce expenses, I had the following: 1. Cut subscriptions, 2. No more eating out, 3. Cheaper apartment, and 4. Cheaper car. There are so many other ideas that come to mind. For example, I stopped clothes shopping for a long time. I reduced my grocery bill by removing things I didn't need, and I lowered my utilities consumption.

This is your brainstorming tool. Take 15 minutes of quiet time by yourself or with your significant other to brainstorm. Jot down all the ideas you can come up with to get out of debt. Let your mind wonder. Be creative. If you later decide you can't go without something you initially wrote down. That's okay. That's for you to decide. This exercise is just to get those thoughts on paper.

This beanstalk illustration works because it demonstrates how important it is to ensure your daily and weekly activities include actions that get you closer to your BIG goals. I am a list person, but if I had looked at some of my to-do lists a few years ago, very rarely would I have found any items that actually related to my BIG goals. Instead, I would have seen all the errands I needed to run or the food I wanted to buy at the grocery store.

If you are a list person, do any of your to-do items tie back to your bigger goals, or are they random one-off things you must get done to get through the day? Something that separates people who achieve big things and people who don't is the focus on their BIG goals. After you've determined your ultimate desires and goals, it's time to figure out what things you can do today to prepare for achieving that BIG goal in the future.

If you want to be a millionaire, it's critical to have goals. Understanding the small, specific steps you need to take today is vital.

Any goal you have can be charted in a beanstalk. If you get stumped on a particular plan, write down what you have and then take a few days off. Let your mind refresh, and then come back to it. Upon coming back to it, you will have thought of a few more ideas. Remember, this is a brainstorming exercise. To write it down in the format actually generates more ideas the longer you sit on it and think about it. You may not even end up using any of the ideas you initially wrote down on your beanstalk. That's okay. The beanstalk tool is not to precisely understand how you will achieve something; instead, it is a tool to generate ideas, to create a more visual image of your desire, and to focus more thoughts on your goal.

Action 3 – Complete Your Beanstalk

Remember, **you don't have to know how you're going to achieve your goal of being debt-free or financially free**. As you continue to think about your goal, ideas will come to you. These ideas create the 'how' to your debt elimination and financial freedom.

This action is one of the most important actions in this entire book. Without a goal, you can take every other action, but you won't change your behavior. You need a target to change your mindset and financial behavior.

For this action, go to www.beanstalkgoals.com[1] and download a free PDF of the *Beanstalk Goals* illustration. This gives you a structure to brainstorm with. Write down your ideas. Remember, your beanstalk doesn't have to be perfect. It's the tool you're using to break your BIG goal into small, actionable steps. You won't know all the steps on day one. As you continue focusing on your big goal, an awesome thing happens. More ideas come to you.

Writing down your goals works. The simple act of organizing your thoughts enough to write them down helps your mind express them outside of your own thinking. Getting those ideas on paper does something for us. It significantly increases our chances of accomplishing the things we want.

Psychology professor at Dominican University, Dr. Gail Matthews, did a study in 2015 to determine how different factors impacted success rates of goals. Success rate grew 42% for participants who wrote down their goals. Per this study, you have a 42% greater chance of achieving your goal if you just write it down.

---

1. http://www.beanstalkgoals.com

Section 2: Regressive Debt
Get Your Hands Dirty

As you've witnessed, your mindset is the foundation. When you've built the right foundation, you're ready for the next priority, your regressive debt.

You may not see anything wrong with debt. Most people see debt as a necessary tool to not only get what they want, but to get through each day.

We have normalized debt in our society. We are bombarded with advertisements for debt daily. Debt is so normal that people who are debt-free are the weird ones. Think about that for a minute. Debt-free people are considered weird. But consider this. We all want financial freedom. We all want enough money to free us from the constraints of our jobs. When you picture yourself becoming financially free, do you see yourself making monthly payments toward debt? I don't think so. I bet you visualize a beach, family, friends, a nice house, or a nice car. You visualize freedom, not someone paying their debt payments.

None of us want to be controlled by anyone. We want to have the freedom to live our life the way we want to live it. We don't want anyone controlling our time, our money, or our beliefs. We are independent and can think for ourselves. If that's so true, why are you letting lenders control your life? With debt, you are obligated to pay it back. To make those payments, you need money. Generally, to have money, you need a job. You're never truly free with debt.

With debt, you won't make the same decisions you'd make without debt. If you have debt, you're likely living paycheck to paycheck. With that pressure on each paycheck, do you ever consider changing jobs?

You may look at other opportunities within your field, but if you're like most people, you won't take a risk in your job because you need this job. You need your paycheck to keep paying your bills. Many people are not happy in their jobs, but with debt they are more likely to feel stuck.

By regressive debt, I'm referring to any debt that is borrowed to purchase depreciating items. This could be a car, camper, clothes, furniture, jewelry, make-up, etc. The moment you purchase any of these items, their value declines. Regressive debt takes you backwards, literally. You cannot have a negative net worth without regressive debt. When you purchase this stuff, you are not only losing the value of the stuff (the price you paid for it), but also you are paying interest on its debt. You're getting hit twice with costs. Regressive debt comes in the form of credit cards, vehicle loans, store financing, payday loans, personal loans, and student loans.

Yes, student loans are a form of regressive debt. I fully recommend investing in yourself and getting an education. Investing in yourself has the highest potential return of all investments. However, taking out tons of student loans isn't the answer. There are alternative ways to get a higher education. Gaining scholarships, attending cheaper schools, and working while you're in school are just a few ideas.

The more student loans you accumulate, the more years you are locking yourself into a job that eats at your time, your life, and potentially your joy. Education should be liberating, not imprisoning.

The Regressive Debt stage takes less time compared to the other stages. You have a whole lifetime in front of you, and regressive debt will not be part of your journey for long.

There are many factors in determining how long it will take you to pay it off, including how much debt you have, how much income you make, and how much spending you will cut. This stage provides a variety of strategies to pay it off. Some strategies will be appealing to you and others will not. I'm going to show you, step-by-step, the actions I took, as well as other strategies I've seen that might appeal to you more.

We are all different. We learn differently. We are motivated differently. Some of us fear numbers and some of us love numbers. Because we are each unique, I don't expect you to do everything exactly as I did it. I know you will create your own path in your own time.

4: Debt has Non-financial Consequences

Debt is baggage you carry with you everywhere you go.

You can't escape it when you go on vacation. You can't escape it when you meet up with your friends. It's always with you, always in the back of your mind, even if you purposefully try to ignore it.

Debt creates negativity in our minds, which eventually manifests itself tangibly in our lives. It starts with feelings of fear, guilt, and shame.

- You might fear being able to pay your bills.
- You might fear getting denied the next time you swipe your card.

- You might feel guilty for having fun while in debt.
- You might feel guilty for accumulating so much debt.

- You might feel ashamed of your current situation.
- You might feel ashamed of not knowing how to improve it.

Why do I know this?

I felt all these emotions when I was drowning in debt. My debt held me back from being open with others. I didn't want people to see what I was going through, so I held up walls and didn't let too many people in.

When we allow debt to create these emotions in our lives, we stay stuck, and we avoid it. Instead of stepping out and taking a risk, we sit back and zone out in front of the television. We numb our pain with shopping, alcohol, medication, caffeine, or sugar. Negative emotions make people want to zone out of their lives to feel better.

I read a story about fear a few years ago which changed how I saw it. The story confirmed there is only space for faith or fear in your mind. There isn't room for both. We have the option to choose faith or fear. Faith is the essence of positivity, and fear is the essence of negativity.

Faith is believing and knowing that what you want, you can have. It's understanding your success at being debt-free already exists. You may not see the path, but it's there waiting for you. I encourage you to choose faith.

Myth 4: You're the Only One Struggling

<u>**The average American has over $90,000 of regressive debt per Bankrate.com.**</u>

You may feel alone, like you're the only one struggling with debt, but given the statistics, you are not alone. We are good at hiding our emotions and utilizing credit, which makes it almost impossible to look at someone and know if they are winning or struggling financially.

This façade we put on each morning doesn't help anyone. We are so driven by our egos and keeping up with Jones' that we assume no one else is experiencing what we're experiencing. We think everyone else has figured it out. We think we're alone. But the numbers don't lie. We have a major debt crisis in America. Everyone is figuring it out as they go.

It's interesting, though, the people who wear the older clothes and drive the older vehicles most likely are doing better financially than the people driving the new cars and wearing the expensive brands.

As Thomas Stanley put it in his book, *The Millionaire Next Door*, "allocating time and money in the pursuit of looking superior often has a predictable outcome: inferior economic achievement."

Too many of us believe we need to look the part and hold up our image, but this isn't true. As Thomas Stanley proved through his research, the vast majority of millionaires and decamillionaires (those with a net worth of greater than $10,000,000) look like everyday people. They don't eat fancy food. They don't drive luxury cars. They don't live in mansions.

I decided years ago this was the person I wanted to be, the person no one would ever suspect is a millionaire. I think I would have gotten away with it too if I didn't have this desire to be a writer.

Emotional Phases

Any time you want to get better at something, it's painful. Think about getting back in shape. Your first few workouts are difficult. You're out of breath. You're sore. This happens for a while until your muscles are conditioned. It's hard at the beginning but eventually gets easier.

Your money is the same. It's going to be hard at first, especially if you're accustomed to living in debt and buying anything you want. You're changing your habits. You're changing your beliefs. Your old habits and beliefs were convenient. These new habits and beliefs are outside your comfort zone.

Let's look at the emotional phases of improving your money. These are especially true for natural spenders.

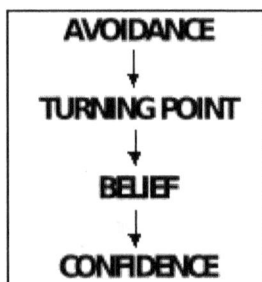

```
┌──────────────────────┐
│      AVOIDANCE        │
│          ↓           │
│    TURNING POINT      │
│          ↓           │
│        BELIEF         │
│          ↓           │
│     CONFIDENCE        │
└──────────────────────┘
```

Avoidance

I was the perfect example of someone in avoidance. After I calculated my net worth and saw it was almost $100,000 negative, I still shopped and swiped my credit card like nothing was wrong. I was stubborn. I thought my income would eventually grow to the level of my spending, and I wouldn't need to worry about it. I was living in a false reality.

Behind my façade, I was stressed and overwhelmed by my growing debt. I didn't want to recognize it. I was ashamed of how negative my net worth was, but it didn't change my spending behavior.

In many cases, negative feelings surface in our lives as avoidance.

- We avoid our statements.
- We avoid talking about money.
- We avoid dealing with our money.

Avoidance doesn't help anything. Have you ever solved a problem by avoiding it? Probably not. The problem most likely got worse.

The only good thing avoidance does is push someone to their turning point.

Turning Point

Your turning point might feel like your bottom. It's the point you decide you're going to change.

My biggest turning point was realizing I was paying $16,000 a year in interest, which you'll see in the next chapter.

Another person's turning point was seeing how much money he made when he did his taxes and having nothing to show for it.

Another person's turning point happened while she was on vacation and went to fill up her tank of gas, and her card was denied. She had maxed out every credit card.

Everyone has slightly different turning points.

Your turning point isn't the bottom though; it's actually the beginning. It's the point where you get angry and frustrated with your behavior. **It's the point you get so fed up that you decide once and for all, you are going to change.**

This is the moment when your money journey starts.

Belief

After you experience the turning point, you are fueled by determination to change.

I know you've felt this feeling before. Think about a time when you felt determined. It might have been a project at work, a relationship, or an athletic competition. Whatever it was, you were determined to succeed.

That is the same drive you feel after this turning point. This determination becomes belief. You believe you can win with money. You believe you can get out of debt. This belief is bigger than hope. This belief is faith. It's knowing you are going to succeed whatever it takes. This belief propels you to create a plan and take action.

Confidence

After you've created a plan and taken action, you'll experience tangible results. Every win you get, no matter how small, builds your confidence. You realize you have the power to make an impact. You see how your behaviors create different outcomes.

This confidence is important. It's this confidence that pushes you through the obstacles and challenges along the way. You know this isn't going to be easy, but when you're confident in your ability to succeed, you will persevere.

Belief, confidence, action, and perseverance are the winning factors for your money.

If you're avoiding your money, know that you're one step away from turning it around.

Pleasure & Pain Drive Your Choices

We as human beings make decisions to seek pleasure and avoid pain. Think about your habits. What are things you do routinely because they provide pleasure?

Do you scroll through social media to see what your friends and family are up to? Do you plan parties with your friends to socialize? Do you cook foods that taste great? These are all pleasure-seeking activities. We all want pleasure in our lives. There's nothing wrong with this. We are meant to enjoy our lives.

However, what happens when the pleasure we seek hurts us? For example, are the foods we eat nutritious, or do we just love the taste, even though they damage our health?

I completely changed my diet a few years ago to avoid the pain of migraines. You might choose to stay in a bad relationship because you can't bear the pain of being alone. You might stay in your comfort zone because you're afraid of the potential pain of failure.

When I think about this pain versus pleasure paradox, I think of a teeter-totter from elementary school. What happens when we think about debt from the pain and pleasure perspective?

When we first get the taste of debt, it feels good. We see debt as a tool to get what we want faster.

You want those new clothes now; why not just open a credit card and get them today instead of waiting for a month until you have the cash?

At this point, you're experiencing immediate gratification. The pleasure you receive from more clothes, more accessories, or a new car outweighs the pain you feel from the monthly payments.

This is illustrated below with the pleasure on top of the pain.

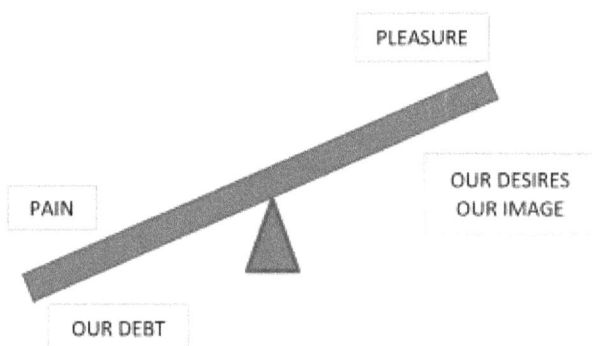

PLEASURE

PAIN

OUR DESIRES
OUR IMAGE

OUR DEBT

As the years go by and the hours of work accumulate, you realize you have a decent salary, but you have very little savings to show for it. The monthly payments never stop. You feel like you're making payments month after month, but your debt isn't going away. The pain of your debt is starting to take a toll. The pain is washing out the pleasure you're getting from spending, as illustrated below where pleasure is now on a similar level as the pain.

At some point, the teeter-totter completely turns the opposite direction. The weight of the debt – the stress, the sleepless nights – has become more painful than the pleasure we get from consuming. The pain of maxing out your credit cards, of barely making the minimum payments, and of worrying if you're approved build up over time.

We finally realize a new pair of shoes isn't going to make us feel better. We finally wake up and realize the only way to get control of our money is to get control of our spending.

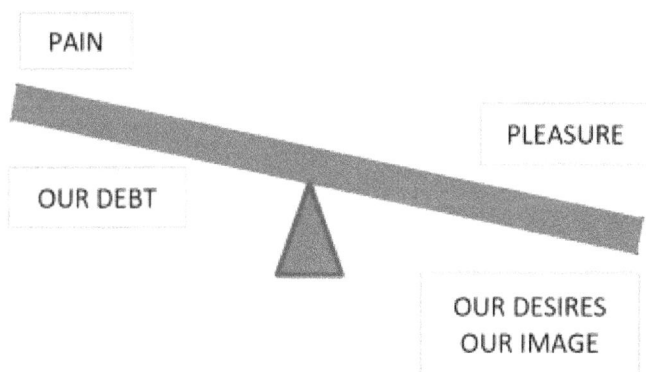

Once you get to this third illustration above, you know it's time to change. You realize if you don't change now, then you are just delaying the inevitable. If you don't change now, you will have to work the rest of your life, or you will have to settle for a very uncomfortable retirement. You've reached your turning point.

I, personally, experienced all three of these phases. If you're a natural saver, you probably didn't learn this the hard way. But, if you're a natural spender like me, then you absolutely understand this.

If you're ready for the advanced level, then this is your teeter-totter below. The pleasure of saving and investing feels much better than the pain of sacrificing your spending.

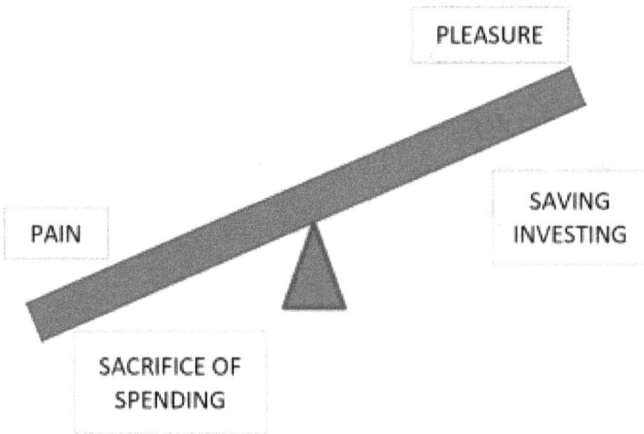

PLEASURE

SAVING
INVESTING

PAIN

SACRIFICE OF
SPENDING

Sacrificing on spending doesn't even feel like sacrifice any longer, because you know your new behaviors are creating a path for you to retire comfortably and early. You can clearly see a path to wealth. That vision is more inspiring than the short-term effects of purchasing less stuff.

Stress is Crippling

In addition to the negative feelings mentioned above, debt causes stress. It never releases you. You might get a new job making more income, but your debt stays with you and eats away at this new income. The stress of the payments and the stress of not feeling in control eats at you every day.

For me, this was the worst part. For years, I knew I had this growing debt, and I let it create uncertainty in my life. I didn't want to know exactly how much of a hole I had created. It seemed easier to avoid it and live my life the way I wanted to live it. If I didn't know the numbers, then I wouldn't need to constrain my spending, is what I thought.

I wish I had woken up sooner. Once I had a plan in place, my stress dissipated. It didn't go away, but it was different. I was taking control of my money. I was taking control of my life.

We are all too familiar with stress. It's become a normal part of our life. Stress is destructive. It not only makes us feel tense, but it's also horrible for our health. When we're stressed, we revert to the 'fight or flight' mode where we are just surviving. Animals have a similar 'fight or flight' mode that happens when a predator is around or they feel threatened, but they are not in this mode all the time. When the threat is gone, they are back to living. When our threats leave, we humans find a way to continue feeling stress through worry. This constant stress increases the size of our amygdala, the part of the brain activated during stress, which creates the opportunity for more stress in the future. Constant stress can also shrink our prefrontal cortex, which is responsible for memory and focus.

When we feel stress, the hormone, cortisol, is released. If we have temporary bouts of stress, cortisol is favorable as it shuts down parts of our bodily functions in order to enhance the bodily functions that will help us in the stressful moment. However, when we feel stress continually, over the long term, cortisol damages our health. Our bodies weren't designed to be under stress all the time. Long term exposure to cortisol creates health issues, including headaches, anxiety, heart disease, and sleep problems.

Don't let your debt harm your health. Don't let the fear of your finances create this constant stress. It's time for action. Action is the cure to fear. It's time to get intentional and take control of your money.

Action 4 – Build Your Boundaries

You may have gotten into this debt on your own, but it's likely your family or friends had a part in it. You wanted to go on a trip with people you love, so you charged it, or you wanted a new outfit for that concert, and you charged it. I'm not saying you should blame anyone for your debt. You've got to own up to your choices. My point is that we are all influenced by the people around us. It's so easy to ignore our own goals and jump into someone else's life. It's easy to prioritize time with friends and family over work. Of course, we would rather spend our time with the people we love than at a job we might not like. It's more fun to go out with our friends than it is to get a part-time job in the evenings. What I'm saying is when you decide you're serious about getting out of debt, it's not only going to impact you, but it's also going to impact those around you.

Your social time with friends might be to shop together, eat out together or get manicures, but some of those expenses will be greatly reduced, if not stopped, to progress to your ultimate vision. Your friends probably won't understand. They may take it personally that you no longer want to spend as much time with them when that's not true. Your debt-free mission has just become a priority over spending frivolously. They may not want to do the free activities you come up with like walking in the park or hanging out at your house. Just a warning, this is going to happen. Not everyone will understand your goal of being debt-free or financially free. Many people believe debt is normal and expect to have it for the rest of their lives. They expect to work until their mid-60's. They don't see any value in sacrificing today.

You're going to get criticized. You may lose some friends over it. It's okay though. You're doing this for you and your family, not for anyone else.

There is a reason they tell you to put your oxygen tank on first if there is an issue with the airplane. You can't help anyone else if you can't breathe. You must first help yourself, and then you are ready to help others.

To help yourself first is to create boundaries for yourself around your spending, your time, and your energy. Write these down. What promises will you make to yourself?

You'll need to prioritize your spending and your time. If you're working more hours to make more income, you're going to have less time to socialize. Prioritize who is most important in your life and who gets those hours you have left to give. Prioritize what is most important to you and only spend money on those things.

These boundaries are for your benefit. Now that you know your true goal, you've got to protect it by creating boundaries around your time and energy. This journey isn't for the faint of heart. Having a strong 'why' is your key to sticking with this.

There are many great outcomes to this though. You find out who your real allies are. The friends and family that stick with you and support you are golden. You'll find out who those people are quickly. You'll also build strong character. Peer pressure is no longer getting the best of you. You got into this mess partially because of peer pressure, but you'll find out how strong you really are. And lastly, once you're in a great financial position, you can help so many others, by either sharing your knowledge or being more generous.

5: Compounding is Magical or Detrimental

We naturally think in straight lines and linearity when it comes to our money. We see our checking account balance grow with each deposit and fall with each expense. Many of us see our retirement accounts the same way. We only count on our contributions to grow the account.

However, depending on what the account is invested in, you won't only see your balance fluctuate with contributions, you will also see it change with the market.

When compounding takes over your money, get ready. You are in for a ride. Compounding happens when you start earning a return, not only on the money you invested, but also on the prior year's returns. Look at this chart below.

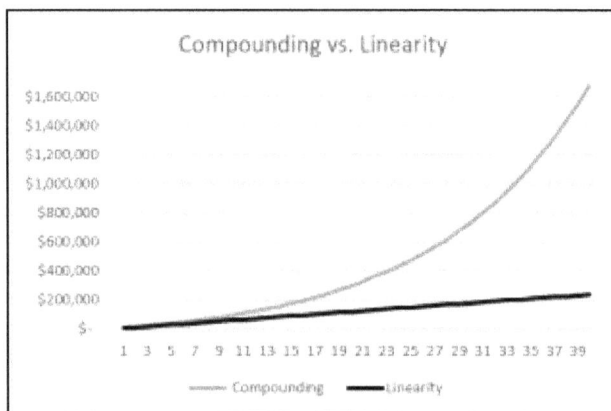

This chart is an example of compounding versus linearity. In both accounts you are contributing $500 a month or $6,000 a year. If you're depositing this into a checking account that makes no interest or putting it under your mattress, the darker line will be the result. At the end of 40 years, you would have $240,000 ($6,000 x 40 years). If you took the same $500 every month and contributed it to an account that averaged an 8% return, then you would end up with over $1,600,000, seven times the amount of the darker line. You can see the first few years don't make much difference between putting the $500 under your mattress or into an investment account, but as time passes and compounding takes effect, the results speak for themselves.

The power of compounding is amazing. Now, the question you should be asking yourself is, *how do I take advantage of this in my life?* That's the right question. How do you get in a position to make compounding work for you?

The first step is to get out of regressive debt. When you're in debt, you're paying interest on the outstanding balance you owe. That interest is working against you, very similar to the compounding example above. It's taking your money at a higher rate than if you were just paying the principal balance back with no interest. The problem is that you are on the wrong side of the equation. Instead of reaping the rewards of compounding, you are paying the price of compounding. Your lender is winning this game.

This is how it works against you. Let's say you have a credit card that charges 18% interest, and you have an outstanding balance of $5,000. If your minimum payment is 5% of your balance, and you pay the minimum payment every month, it will take you 14 years to pay this off, and you'll pay over $2,000 in interest. That means that whatever you bought to create that $5,000 balance is now costing you $7,000. Would you have been willing to pay 40% more for those items? That's, in essence, what you've done. You've paid $7,000 for those items instead of the price tag of $5,000 because of the interest. Compounding is not your friend if you have regressive debt.

I mentioned I was a loan officer for a few years. This was my first experience interacting with customers and their money. I remember a customer whose vehicle had been repossessed. He was making payments to the bank on the difference between his loan value and the amount the bank was able to sell his vehicle for at auction. The remaining balance was around $6,000 at a 15% interest rate. In other words, this debt was generating about $75 of interest every month ($6,000 *0.15/12), but he was only making payments of $25 a month. He wasn't covering the interest with his payments, which meant every month his loan balance grew by $50, and then $50.63, $51.26, $51.90, etc. Because this customer's monthly payments weren't covering the interest on this loan, the principal balance kept growing every month. This is real compounding working the wrong way.

Let's focus instead on the positive power of compounding. The goal is to get yourself in a position to receive the benefits, not pay the price.

Myth 5: Interest Rates have Little Impact

Interest rates are the key to understanding your money better.

Interest rates create the magical phenomenon, compounding, we just saw. If you invest, compound interest will make you wealthy. If you're in debt, compound interest will create a financial disaster.

Let's look at a common example, a car loan. On a $20,000 loan at a 5% interest rate, you would pay about $83 a month in interest ($20,000*0.05/12). That doesn't include the principal payback. That is only the cost to borrow the money. That $83 disappears from your account every month. Think of what you could do with $83 extra dollars every month. It may not sound like a lot, but that could be your cable bill or your cell phone bill. We tend to get angry when the cable company increases our bill, but at the same time we are paying hundreds of dollars in interest every month, which doesn't seem to bother us.

Interest gets very expensive as you borrow more. We are only talking about $20,000 above. What if you had a $75,000 student loan with an average interest rate of 10%? You would be paying $625 a month in interest alone ($75,000*0.10/12). That is a lot of money! Again, that $625 you pay each month wouldn't cover any of your principal balance. It would only cover the interest expense. In other words, if you paid $625 every month, at the end of the year you would have made $7,500 in payments, but your debt balance would still be $75,000. You would have made all those payments but not made a dent in your debt balance – talk about nil progress even though you worked a lot of hours to make the interest-only payments.

Let's revisit that first example to understand the other side of compound interest. If you invested just $83 each month and left it in an index fund averaging a 10% return per year, after just 10 years, you'd have $17,000 (but you would have only contributed $10,000). After 20 years, you'd have $62,000 (but you would have only contributed $20,000). When you have extra cash to invest, you are putting yourself in a position to let compounding work for you.

The Beginning

As I mentioned earlier, I was one of those people who graduated with a lot of student loan debt. To make it worse, I purchased a rental property and eventually a fixer-upper to live in.

In terms of the stages, my mindset was completely skewed, my regressive debt was out of control, I had very little in retirement, and I had progressive debt. I was in too many stages at once and not making progress in any of them.

Finally at age 31, I got serious about improving my financial situation. I listed out all my debts with their interest rates and balances to get an estimate of what I was paying. With my student loans, credit cards, and mortgages, it totaled around $235,000 worth of debt – not a surprise there.

Just a quick sidebar; I had another $25,000 of student loans but had cashed out my 401k to pay this loan off just a few months before doing this exercise. That's how I came up with the total $260,000 in debt in the *Introduction*.

Closing that 401k was another bad move, as I know now. All the financial experts say, 'don't cash out your retirement.' I know, you might be asking yourself, *why I am listening to this author – she's made every mistake in the book*. That's exactly why you should keep listening. I've made just about every financial mistake you can think of and still came out on top. I've done so many dumb things with my money and still managed to become a millionaire. I want these examples to emphasize how possible this is for you too. You are likely already so far ahead of where I was.

I then calculated how much interest I was paying every year. Figuring out my annual interest expense became not only another turning point, but the turning point for me.

Debts	Balance	Monthly	Interest Rate	Annual Interest
Credit Card 1	$2,500	$100	18.00%	$450
Credit Card 2	$18,917	$397	13.99%	$2,646
Credit Card 3	$0	$100	18.99%	$0
Duplex Mortgage	$44,766	$465	6.50%	$2,910
Residence Mortgage	$51,778	$407	4.30%	$2,226
Student Loan 1	$30,817	$160	3.25%	$1,002
Student Loan 2	$41,931	$306	8.50%	$3,564
Student Loan 3	$22,304	$156	6.80%	$1,517
Student Loan 4	$21,494	$156	6.80%	$1,462
Total Debt	**$234,507**	**$2,247**		**$15,777**

It astounded me when I did the calculation. I knew my student loan rates were high, but I never imagined I was paying almost $16,000 a year in interest. I was throwing away $16,000 every year! I could not believe this. No wonder my debt balances weren't declining as fast as I wanted; most of my payments were going straight to interest and not impacting the principal balance much at all.

Full disclosure: at this time my take-home pay was around $48,000. This meant one-third of my take-home pay was being wasted on interest. No wonder my debt wasn't getting smaller.

I was making all my payments on time, and nothing was happening. The debt wasn't going away. By calculating this interest expense, I finally saw exactly what was happening.

This was eye-opening for me. Remember in the first chapter, the *Ignorance Isn't Bliss* section? When you haven't written down your total balances and interest rates, you are living in ignorance. You don't really know your total debt, and I bet you don't have a clue what you are paying in interest every year.

When you don't know where you are, it's difficult to go where you want to go. If you don't know the starting point for your GPS, how do you expect your GPS to get you to your destination? If you want to get out of debt, that is your destination. However, to accomplish this goal, you need to figure out where you are today.

As I mentioned above, my take-home pay was around $48,000. My total monthly debt payments were $2,247 (see above table), which equates to about $27,000 per year ($2,247 * 12 = $27,000). Take a minute to think about these percentages. More than 50% of my take home pay was going straight to debt payments. ($27,000 / $48,000 = 56%)

As you know most debt payments are partially interest payments and partially principal payments. My annual interest was $16,000, meaning my principal payments were around $11,000.

In percentage terms, this is where my paycheck was going:

- 33% interest on debt
- 23% debt principal payments
- 34% living expenses
- 10% retirement investing

What finally clicked for me was the amount of money I could invest if I didn't have debt. I could invest 56% of my take-home pay if I could pay off these debts.

This was the game changer. This is what pushed me to go all-in to pay off my debt.

Action 5 – List Your Debts & Calculate Your Annual Interest

List all your debt balances, including credit cards, collections, car loans, student loans, payday loans, personal loans, business loans, and real estate loans. Add their interest rate as well as their monthly payment and calculate your annual interest expense.

Annual Interest Expense = Interest Rate x Total Debt Balance

I know this can be hard. You need to physically find your statements and figure out all the open accounts you have. It is likely more difficult because you fear what this list will tell you. You fear the unknown. I experienced this exact feeling. Avoiding the problem only makes it worse though.

Writing it down is the only way you can move forward. If you don't know how much debt you have or how many accounts you have open or how much interest you're paying, how can you expect to make progress? Knowledge is golden. The more knowledge you have, the better you can devise a strategy to conquer it.

You can create your own or download the free Microsoft Excel template at https://winwithyourmoney.com/free-template.

Whatever format allows you to see your debt position clearly is the right format for you. Start updating this file at least once a month. Create a habit of looking at this routinely throughout the year. This step allows you to see exactly where you are. You may have a similar reaction when you see how much your debt adds up to or how much interest you are paying every year.

This could be your wake-up call. Don't skip this step. Ignorance is not bliss. Ignorance is avoidance. If you avoid your fears and never face them, you won't dig yourself out of any holes. You won't grow, and you won't move forward. Face your fear, take the time, and do this due diligence upfront.

For me, this was my second turning point, and I made major changes.

Focus

This may sound counterintuitive, but now that you've written out all your debts, it's time to choose one debt to start with.

The act of writing down all your accounts, your total balances, and the interest rates gives you the perspective of flying over the forest. You can see everything clearly now.

When you focus on one account and have tunnel vision within that account, the results are compounded and achieved much faster.

Tunnel vision is critical in paying off your regressive debt. Tunnel vision is laser focus on your goal. I was reminded of tunnel vision the other day when I went to the grocery store. I didn't have much time but needed two items from this large store. Luckily, I knew exactly where these items were. As I walked in the direction of these items, I realized how easily it could be to get distracted. There were many things on display that I was tempted to stop and look at. I think this happens to many of us. We set a goal, and then instead of focusing on it, we get distracted with life, work, family, and other responsibilities and lose any tunnel vision we may have had.

Focusing on a goal creates more thoughts around this goal. Have you ever noticed when your thoughts are dominated by a problem that the solution comes to you later, maybe in the shower or before you go to bed? When your thoughts are dominated by one topic, that topic saturates your mind. Your mind goes to work without you even realizing it. Your mind is working behind the scenes, creating ideas and solutions to your thoughts.

Quick sidenote: make sure you continue paying the minimum monthly payments on all other debt accounts. Incurring additional fees on other debts would only make your journey more difficult.

Now you may be asking, *how do I choose which account to pay off first?*

There are two well-known methods: the debt snowball and the debt avalanche.

Debt Snowball or Debt Avalanche

The debt-snowball was coined by Dave Ramsey in his book, *The Total Money Makeover*. To follow this method, start with the debt that has the smallest balance first.

It doesn't matter if this is a credit card, a student loan, a car loan, a personal loan, or a collection. What matters is the total debt balance. Find the smallest total balance you have and focus all your attention on this account.

The debt snowball works because in many cases, you can pay off your smallest debt quickly, maybe in a month or two. This is a quick win. You have tangible progress you can see.

This quick win translates into confidence. When you see results from your new behaviors, you gain confidence. Confidence provides motivation and gives you the ability to persevere when things get difficult.

We need to see progress, or we become unmotivated very quickly. Think about the last time you tried to lose weight or started a new habit. If you didn't see progress within a few weeks, I bet you gave up. We need small wins. Small wins give us inspiration and create consistency in our new habits.

Depending on how much debt you have, this could be a long journey. Mine was almost five years. Anything that gives you a head-start, such as paying off the smallest balance first is powerful. It sets the stage for the rest of your journey.

The second method is the debt avalanche. This method starts by paying off the debt account with the highest interest rate.

I'm a numbers person at heart, so I was naturally driven by the interest rate. The interest rate is the cost you're paying to borrow this money. Debts with higher interest rates cost more.

Mathematically, this is the quickest method. You pay off your highest-cost account first, which saves money in the long run.

This illustration shows the difference between these two strategies. Following the debt snowball, you would go after the $1,500 credit card balance first. Using the debt avalanche, you would go after the $5,000 credit card balance first.

Debt Snowball

Debt	Total Balance	Interest Rate
Credit Card 1	$ 1,500	9%
Credit Card 2	$ 5,000	22%
Student Loan	$ 6,700	4%
Vehicle Loan	$ 9,500	10%

Debt Avalanche

Debt	Total Balance	Interest Rate
Credit Card 2	$ 5,000	22%
Vehicle Loan	$ 9,500	10%
Credit Card 1	$ 1,500	9%
Student Loan	$ 6,700	4%

This is your journey. Pay off your accounts in the order that feels right to you. Recall, your money is connected to every aspect of your life, including your emotions. If you choose a strategy that doesn't intuitively feel right, then this journey will be more difficult than it needs to be.

Use your emotions and feelings to your benefit. If you're doubting yourself and whether you can really pay off your debt, then start with your smallest account. Watch your progress unfold as you pay off that first debt.

If you've had it and are completely committed to getting out of debt no matter what, then start with the highest-interest debt.

6: Debt is a Puzzle to be Hacked

It's easy to get overwhelmed by your debt, especially if you have no idea where to start. It's natural to attach negative feelings to this debt, but I want to challenge you again to change your perspective. Instead of focusing on the negatives around your debt, see it as a puzzle to be figured out.

Make it a game – a challenge, nothing more. The facts are you got yourself into this debt, and you can get yourself out. Today, however, you are smarter. You have a better understanding of money. You have more control over your ego and more willpower over your spending. You've gained awareness of the credit industry. You will no longer fall for their tricks.

Seeing life as a game and your goal as a puzzle makes it fun. Too many people let these burdens destroy them. Instead, stop taking it so seriously. Yes, you made some bad decisions. You now know where those bad decisions led you, and you don't like where you are. The good news is you learned a lesson, and you're ready to move forward.

When you see your goals as puzzles, the entire process becomes a challenge and less of a burden. You know what you want and why you want it. You're more likely to go for it. You're less likely to fear failure.

Myth 6: Retail Credit Cards are a Good Deal

<u>**You spend more when you think you're getting a good deal.**</u>

With all the points, rewards, and perks you're getting with your retail store credit cards, how could I say these credit cards aren't a good deal?

Ever notice how inspired to spend you are when you think you're getting a good deal? I have one store in mind which created their own currency. You get their cash when you spend money at their store. And when you spend more money, you get more of their cash. The caveat is their cash isn't redeemable anywhere else. You only get the benefits of having their cash when you spend more at their stores. Do you see the cycle many people are trapped in?

This rewards system as well as the plethora of coupons provided by other stores are a physical reminder of your potential savings the next time you go shopping. Every time you look in your wallet, you're reminded of that coupon. You may even have the expiration dates memorized.

Companies know what fuels consumers to act. Urgency, which is given by the expiration date, is a big reason for spending. The other is loyalty and deals. When we have a specific store's credit card, we are more likely to continue shopping at that store instead of a competitor.

When we have physical coupons in our wallet, we are reminded every time we look in our wallet that this deal is waiting for us.

What if you decided to escape this cycle and put something else in your wallet that would push you in a different direction?

Visuals

I'm sure you've heard of a vision board. These became popular with the book, *The Secret*, over a decade ago. Vision boards work. The idea is to create a poster, paper, corkboard, or whiteboard with photos of what you want. This could be people, real estate, investments, cars, companies, whatever you desire in your future. Place this somewhere you can see it each day, either on a wall or in your wallet. The visual impressions you make over and over as you look at it each day renews your focus and aligns your subconscious mind with your conscious mind.

You've seen charitable fundraisers use a thermometer to show how much progress they've made on their goal. Many kids around the world use a paper chain to count down the days until Christmas. We use visuals a lot when we're trying to achieve a goal.

Use visuals like these to show your progress on paying off your debt and becoming financially free. Instead of looking at coupons in your wallet which tempt you to shop, add a card that shows your progress on your debt-pay-off journey or a quote or picture that reminds you why you're doing this.

My vision board consists of a hodgepodge of pieces of paper. There are pictures of people I love. There are quotes. There are emails I was excited to receive. I also have a map of an island I visited a few years ago, which turned out to be my favorite trip of all time. I have other maps of hiking trails that I'd like to return to.

There is no wrong answer when it comes to your vision board. I wouldn't expect two people to have the exact same vision board given how different each one of us is. As you determine what you truly want in life, add pictures, quotes, maps, emails, or whatever you have to your vision board to keep you on track.

Refinancing Higher Interest to Lower Rates

Seeing my annual interest expense was the wake-up call I needed. And because of this, my goal was to reduce that interest expense as much as possible. Every dollar that went toward interest was a dollar that couldn't pay down the principal balance.

Refinancing was one tool I used to get tangible reductions on my annual interest expense. With all the credit options we have today, there are opportunities to lower your interest expense.

One of my first moves was to refinance my primary residence to a lower rate. Because I had built some equity in my fixer upper, I was able to do a cash-out refinance, which meant I took out a higher loan value on the house, giving me extra cash to pay toward my high-interest credit cards. I partially paid off Credit Card 2 at 13.99% and transferred it to my new mortgage at 3.25%. My mortgage rate went from 4.3% to 3.25% as well.

The next move I made was to take a loan out on my paid-off vehicle. I was paying 18% on Credit Card 1 and 13.99% on Credit Card 2. I paid off these credit cards and opened a new vehicle loan at 5.5%, saving a lot in interest.

Those two moves – refinancing my house and my car – lowered my annual interest from $15,800 to $13,100.

Many financial experts tell you not to consolidate like this. Their logic is sound. What I did was take unsecured debt (the credit cards) and move it to secured debt (my house and my car). In other words, I took more risk for these debts. I was morally obligated to pay those debts anyway. It didn't matter if the debt was on credit cards or on my house. I was committed to paying it off, and I wanted it to be at the cheapest price.

If you're not fully committed to paying off your debt, then consolidating a credit card balance into your mortgage is not the right thing for you. If you're not fully committed, then you won't actually close that credit card; you'll continue spending on it and will find yourself with a high credit card balance again in the near future. Don't take this action if you're not 100% committed to getting out of debt.

Below was my financial picture five months later. My annual interest expense was down by $2,700.

Remember, it takes time to make significant progress. I know you likely aren't impressed with my results in these first five months, but I was planting seeds early on. I was focusing on minimizing my interest, so when I started making big payments on my debt, these payments would make a bigger impact.

Focus on planting the seeds of your journey, putting in the work early by planning even though you won't see the results immediately. It takes time to grow crops, just like it takes time for your efforts to produce tangible results.

Debts	Balance	Monthly	Interest Rate	Annual Interest
Credit Card 1	$0	$0	18.00%	$0
Credit Card 2	$0	$0	13.99%	$0
Credit Card 3	$0	$0	18.99%	$0
Duplex Mortgage	$44,766	$465	6.50%	$2,910
Residence Mortgage	$64,000	$447	3.25%	$2,080
Vehicle Loan	$10,000	$307	5.50%	$550
Student Loan 1	$30,817	$160	3.25%	$1,002
Student Loan 2	$41,931	$306	8.50%	$3,564
Student Loan 3	$22,304	$156	6.80%	$1,517
Student Loan 4	$21,494	$156	6.80%	$1,462
Total Debt	**$235,312**	**$1,997**		**$13,084**

When you refinance, make sure you not only compare the impact of the interest rate reduction but also the associated fees. In many cases to refinance a vehicle, there is a $200 to $500 loan fee, and there may also be a prepayment penalty if you pay it off too early. To refinance your house, the fees can range from $500 to $5,000, or even more. Be on the look-out for these fees and make sure they are part of your calculation.

To ensure a refinance is the right option for you, plug your numbers into this equation below to see how much savings you should expect.

Principal Balance	x	Current Interest Rate	x	Number of Years to Pay Off	>	Principal Balance	x	New Interest Rate	x	Number of Years to Pay Off	+	Loan Origination Fees	+	Prepayment Penalty

In words, the **Principal Balance** (the value of the loan of you want to refinance) times the **Current Interest Rate** times the **Number of Years Remaining to Pay Off this Debt** must be greater than the **Principal Balance** times the **New Interest Rate** times the **Number of Years to Pay Off** plus the **Loan Origination and Prepayment Fees**.

Using just addition and multiplication, you can put your numbers into this formula and see if refinancing is the best option for you.

Just a heads-up, this formula is a simplified version, rounded to years. If you want to get fancy and put these values into a spreadsheet, you can calculate this by month, getting you a more accurate number. For the decision though, this formula picks up all the variables and will give you the right answer. Keep it simple when you can.

Let's look at my real-life example.

Principal Balance	x	Current Interest Rate	x	Number of Years to Pay Off	>	Principal Balance	x	New Interest Rate	x	Number of Years to Pay Off	+	Loan Origination Fees	+	Prepayment Penalty
$ 10,000	x	13.99%	x	3	>	$ 10,000	x	5.50%	x	3	+	$ 300	+	$

		$ 4,197	>	$ 1,950	

I took out a $10,000 loan on my car at 5.5% to partially pay off a credit card at 13.99%. My loan fees were $300, and there were no prepayment penalties. I saved around $2,247 ($4,197 - $1,950) because of this refinance. This might not seem like much money over three years, but it was moves like this that created significant reductions in my interest and debt. Every dollar saved matters, especially when you have a big pile of debt.

Get creative. This can include any debt: your mortgage, car loan, student loans, or boat loan. Talk to your local banker and search well-known websites for good deals. If you can wipe away some of your annual interest expenses, the debt will go away much faster.

Don't put yourself in a worse position though. If the math doesn't work or comes out to a savings of less than $100, it's probably not worth the hassle. You're trying to reduce your interest expenses, but at the same time, you want to keep things simple. When you start adding complexity to your loan arrangements, things can spiral out of control quickly.

Selling Anything You Don't Need

Look around. Do you have an extra car? Can you downsize in vehicle or house? Is there a boat, motorcycle, or camper that rarely gets used? Do you have anything of value that could be sold online? Do you have a rental property that isn't making much income?

When you sell things, the profit goes straight to the principal of your debt balances. If you sell something that has debt on it, you can pay off that debt immediately and may have additional funds to pay other debts down. That's a win-win.

If you decide you don't have anything of value to sell, that's okay. Do a quick purge anyway. Throw away or donate anything you no longer use. Why keep around stuff you don't use? Getting rid of stuff feels great. It's freeing to let go of things. Remember, getting control of your money is interconnected to all other aspects of your life. Freeing yourself of physical clutter is a great way to clear your mind and create more focused thoughts on getting out of debt.

At this point in my life, I had just bought a house and didn't have much to sell other than a duplex. This duplex ended up being a nightmare for me. I evicted tenants, delt with intentional damage, and didn't make any money. It was time for this property to be sold, along with all the stress that came with it. Selling this property didn't happen immediately though.

It sat on the market for over a year. I made the mistake of hiring a real estate agent with no experience in selling rentals. We finally agreed to split ways, and I found another real estate agent who was able to sell it quickly. After being listed on the market for fourteen months, the duplex sold for $8,000 less than the original purchase price. I paid $68,000 for it in 2009 and sold it for $60,000 in 2013. These values may seem surprisingly low given where real estate is today, but this was right after the 2008 housing crises, and the property was in a very rural area in the Midwest. Even though I made a ton of mistakes in how I bought and managed this property, I did a few things right. I had taken out a 15-year fixed-rate mortgage and paid on it for four years. Because of this, I received a check for around $9,000 at the closing.

With those funds, I was able to pay off more of that high-interest student loan debt, eliminating even more annual interest expense. I had also received multiple zero-percent credit card offers in the mail and took full advantage of those. I was down to $6,500 in annual interest expense, and my debt was down to $177,000, primarily driven by the sale of the duplex.

Debts	Balance	Monthly	Interest Rate	Annual Interest
Credit Card 1	$2,957	$100	15.00%	$ 444
Credit Card 2	$17,920	$397	0.00%	$ -
Credit Card 3	$5,382	$100	0.00%	$ -
Credit Card 4	$8,300	$100	0.00%	$ -
Residence Mortgage	$62,366	$448	3.25%	$ 2,027
Vehicle Loan	$8,619	$307	4.99%	$ 430
Student Loan 1	$29,532	$160	2.63%	$ 775
Student Loan 2	$0	$0	8.50%	$ -
Student Loan 3	$21,623	$156	6.80%	$ 1,470
Student Loan 4	$20,138	$156	6.80%	$ 1,369
Total Debt	**$176,837**	**$1,924**		**$ 6,515**

You may not have been impressed with my progress after five months but look at what happened a little over a year into the journey. A decision I made in the prior year regarding the selling of the duplex finally paid off.

Plant those seeds.

Put in the work and planning upfront and stick with your goal. You might not see the results you want immediately, but that doesn't mean your actions aren't working. Results take time. The more consistent and focused you are, the more powerful the results will be when they come.

Zero-Percent Credit Card Deals

Another creative tool I used was zero-percent credit card deals. The key to receiving these great offers from your credit card company is having excellent credit. Not everyone has these opportunities, but if you do, consider these as an option.

What is a zero-percent credit card deal? These deals are exactly what they sound like. Your credit card company will reach out to you and either physically send you blank checks or email you an offer where you can transfer higher-interest debt onto your credit card balances. You treat these blank checks like a payment toward your other loan. The credit card company will charge you zero percent interest for a specific period of time.

You may think interest rates have risen recently, and these are no longer available. However, in July 2023 I received a zero percent offer from my credit card company. These are still available today.

The zero-percent credit card offers I used were only good for 12-to-18 months. I knew I only had 12-to-18 months to pay these off or the interest on $31,602 (below three balances $17,920 + $5,382 + $8,300) would skyrocket. The only way to continue making progress on this debt was to pay it off quickly and within the specified terms.

Below is a copy from above, highlighting Credit Cards 2, 3, and 4, the zero-percent interest accounts.

Debts	Balance	Monthly	Interest Rate	Annual Interest
Credit Card 1	$2,957	$100	15.00%	$ 444
Credit Card 2	$17,920	$397	0.00%	$ -
Credit Card 3	$5,382	$100	0.00%	$ -
Credit Card 4	$8,300	$100	0.00%	$ -
Residence Mortgage	$62,366	$448	3.25%	$ 2,027
Vehicle Loan	$8,619	$307	4.99%	$ 430
Student Loan 1	$29,532	$160	2.63%	$ 775
Student Loan 2	$0	$0	8.50%	$ -
Student Loan 3	$21,623	$156	6.80%	$ 1,470
Student Loan 4	$20,138	$156	6.80%	$ 1,369
Total Debt	**$176,837**	**$1,924**		**$ 6,515**

Paying zero percent interest meant 100% of my monthly payment went toward the principal balance. I didn't have to worry about 20% or 30%

going toward interest, because the entire monthly payment was applied to the principal.

Paying down the principal gets you so much further than throwing away money toward interest. When you pay down the principal, you actually make progress on your debt.

Who can beat zero-percent interest? These are great deals, but the credit card companies know that not everyone is on top of their finances, and people get distracted. This is where the companies make their money, from those who stop paying attention. Don't let this be you.

Keep these facts in mind if you decide zero-percent credit cards are a good option for you.

- **There will be a transfer fee.**

There is almost always a transfer fee involved in transferring the balance from your loan to your zero-percent credit card. The credit card companies can't take on all the risk, and to compensate they charge a fee to take on this balance. That's okay though; this can still be a win-win for you.

Make sure you add this fee into your balance. For example, if your credit card limit is $10,000 with a fee of 3%, it's probably a good idea not to transfer more than $9,500. The transfer fee would then be $9,500 times 3% or $285. That means your balance would be $9,785 after the transfer occurs, which is getting close to your total limit of $10,000.

Use the same calculation we looked at previously when comparing loans at different interest rates. Even though the credit card is a zero-percent offer, the fee might outweigh the benefits. Put the balance you intend to transfer into the formula as the Principal Balance and compare the interest and the fees. In this example, you'll save almost $400.

Principal Balance		Current Interest Rate		Number of Years to Pay Off		Principal Balance		New Interest Rate		Number of Years to Pay Off		Loan Origination Fees		Prepayment Penalty
$ 9,500	x	6.80%	x	1	>	$ 9,500	x	0.00%	x	1	+	$ 285	+	$ -

$ 646	>	$ 285	

- **Check the term of the zero interest.**

You need to know how long the zero-interest deal lasts. Mine were generally 12-to-18 months. This is the only way you will know how much to transfer. If you don't think you can pay it off within that term, then don't transfer as much. They will tack on interest if you can't pay it off completely within the specified term. Only transfer as much as you can definitely pay off within the term of the zero-percent period.

For example, if the term of the zero-interest deal is 12 months, and you can pay $1,000 per month on this $9,785 balance, then you are good. You'll have it paid off in 10 months. However, if you only have $500 available to pay each month, then don't transfer this entire balance. Instead, transfer only $5,000 or less. This will give you a bit of cushion in case something comes up in the next 12 months.

- **Only use cards that don't have an existing balance to transfer balances to.**

If you have any existing balance on your credit card, that balance will continue to be charged at the regular 15%-29% interest rate while you are paying 0% on the transferred balance only. The credit card company will apply your monthly payments to the 0% portion instead of the high-interest portion.

Let's say you have $2,000 outstanding on a credit card at 20% interest and you transfer a balance of $5,000 at 0%. You'll continue to get a $33 ($2,000 * 20%/12) interest charge every month, and the new payments you make will be applied to the $5,000 zero-percent balance only, meaning you'll need to pay off the entire $5,000 before any payments are applied to the high-interest balance on your card.

- **If you decide to transfer a balance to one of your cards, put this card in a safe place, like a filing cabinet or desk, somewhere you cannot easily access it.**

You do not want to accidentally use this card while you're paying off your 0% balance. If you do use it, again, that purchase will be charged at the higher interest rate, and your monthly payments will be applied to the zero-percent balance. Therefore, that accidental purchase will likely end up costing you double what you paid for it.

If you follow the above advice and stay focused, you can save a ton of money with these offers. These steps made a dramatic difference in how quickly I was able to pay off my debt. I ended up using multiple zero-percentage offers to save on interest. I saved over $10,000 in interest during my debt-free journey just by using these deals.

The below table shows how closely I managed these cards. This was year four of my five-year debt-free journey, and I had four zero-percent credit cards going at the same time. I wrote out all the balances, the month of the transfer, and the estimated date when I could get their balance to zero. I had $2,300 to pay toward the cards every month. Knowing this helped me to understand how much in total I could transfer and pay off by the end of the zero-percent term.

	Card 1 Balance	Card 1 Pmt	Card 2 Balance	Card 2 Pmt	Card 3 Balance	Card 3 Pmt	Card 4 Balance	Card 4 Pmt	Total CC pmts
June	$ 16,600		$ 3,300		$ 7,800	$	$ -		$ -
July	$ 15,600	$ (1,000)	$ 3,200	$ (100)	$ 7,700	$ (100)	$ 6,500		$ (1,200)
Aug	$ 14,600	$ (1,000)	$ 3,100	$ (100)	$ 7,600	$ (100)	$ 6,400	$ (100)	$ (1,300)
Sept	$ 13,600	$ (1,000)	$ 3,000	$ (100)	$ 7,500	$ (100)	$ 6,300	$ (100)	$ (1,300)
Oct	$ 11,600	$ (2,000)	$ 2,900	$ (100)	$ 7,400	$ (100)	$ 6,200	$ (100)	$ (2,300)
Nov	$ 9,600	$ (2,000)	$ 2,800	$ (100)	$ 7,300	$ (100)	$ 6,100	$ (100)	$ (2,300)
Dec	$ 7,600	$ (2,000)	$ 2,700	$ (100)	$ 7,200	$ (100)	$ 6,000	$ (100)	$ (2,300)
Jan	$ 5,600	$ (2,000)	$ 2,600	$ (100)	$ 7,100	$ (100)	$ 5,900	$ (100)	$ (2,300)
Feb	$ 3,600	$ (2,000)	$ 2,500	$ (100)	$ 7,000	$ (100)	$ 5,800	$ (100)	$ (2,300)
Mar	$ 1,600	$ (2,000)	$ 2,400	$ (100)	$ 6,900	$ (100)	$ 5,700	$ (100)	$ (2,300)
April	$ -	$ (1,600)	$ 2,300	$ (100)	$ 6,400	$ (500)	$ 5,600	$ (100)	$ (2,300)
May			$ 2,200	$ (100)	$ 4,300	$ (2,100)	$ 5,500	$ (100)	$ (2,300)
June			$ 2,100	$ (100)	$ 2,200	$ (2,100)	$ 5,400	$ (100)	$ (2,300)
July			$ 300	$ (1,800)	$ 1,800	$ (400)	$ 5,300	$ (100)	$ (2,300)
Aug			$ -	$ (300)	$ 800	$ (1,000)	$ 4,300	$ (1,000)	$ (2,300)
Sept					$ -	$ (800)	$ 2,800	$ (1,500)	$ (2,300)
Oct							$ 500	$ (2,300)	$ (2,300)
Nov							$ -	$ (500)	$ (500)

Ignorance may have gotten me into debt, but as you can see, intentionality got me out. I started being intentional with every dollar I spent. I started focusing on how much I could pay off every paycheck. It became a challenge I couldn't resist. This challenge was motivation for me to do this.

Action 6 – Create a Budget

Creating a budget is like creating boundaries in your life. Boundaries are a good thing. They keep you in a range of behavior that gives stability and protection. When you let others impede your boundaries, you are disrespecting yourself and your goals. You're not staying true to the promises you made to yourself.

A budget represents your financial boundaries. It shows that you respect yourself enough to create a plan for your future. A budget isn't a prison. It's a guiding post. You are setting the boundaries on your spending just like you set other boundaries in your life.

Stop associating a budget with something negative. It's a tool that helps you become aware of your spending and provides the ability to get control of your spending. Its job isn't to stop you from spending. Its job is for you to become aware of how much you're spending. You are the author of your budget. You control how much is spent where. A budget doesn't take away control, it empowers you.

The nuts and bolts of the budget come down to two levers: income and expenses.

1. **Figure out how much income you have coming in each month.**

Do you have a steady income each month? Do you have multiple sources of income? Or does your income fluctuate?

Write down all your sources of income. If your income varies, write in your average monthly income.

1. **Determine your total monthly expenses.**

Write down all your expenses starting with your needs. Many budgets start like this:

- Housing (rent, insurance, property taxes, utilities, HOA)
- Transportation (gas, insurance)
- Food
- Other (kids, phone, pets, clothes, entertainment, subscriptions, memberships, travel, gifts, office supplies, hobbies, etc.)
- Next, write down all your minimum monthly debt payments (student loans, credit cards, car loans, personal loans, etc).

The first time you put together your budget, it's going to be messy and potentially frustrating. It's going to take longer, but don't let this deter you from doing it. I promise it gets easier each month you put it together.

The first budget is the most difficult because you don't know how much you spend on clothes, groceries, kids, etc. A great way to get a good estimate is to look at your prior months' transactions. When you see what you spent in the prior two months, you can estimate much better.

Remember, you are the author of your budget. Once you've seen your prior month actual spending, you have the ability to cut in areas that don't provide value. You also have the power to add in areas that do provide value. You get to make these decisions, and by putting together a budget, you get to make these decisions intentionally instead of just spending without a plan.

Once you've added up your total income and total expenses, compare your income to your expenses. If your total expenses are higher than your total income, you have some work to do immediately. Your first goal is to get your income higher than your expenses.

If your expenses are less than your income, then you have some flexibility based on how quickly you want to get out of debt.

You are 100% in control of your expenses. You develop this budget based on how quickly you want to get out of debt. If you want to eradicate this debt as fast as possible, then you've got to live on as little as possible. If you aren't willing to sacrifice everything, then create your budget in that way.

This is your personalized budget, no one else's. You define the boundaries and set the targets.

7: Let's Get Lean

You've made the commitment. You are going to pay off your debt and become a millionaire. As we just saw in the budget, there are two primary levers when getting control of your money – income and expenses.

To propel this process forward, it's vital that you minimize your expenses in the short run. This isn't permanent; it's just a temporary change to reap the rewards of being debt-free in the long run.

I cut a ton of expenses on my journey. I basically stopped clothes shopping. I remember needing a pair of tennis shoes but didn't want to spend much money. I went to the clearance rack. They didn't have my size, so I purchased a pair of shoes half size too small. They were marked down dramatically, and that's what mattered. They weren't comfortable. My toes were cramped every time I worked out, but instead of being upset by this, I used it as a reminder of my goal. Today, this seems extreme, but back then I was so fired up about getting out of debt, it didn't matter.

You don't have to go this far. This was a choice I made because I wanted to be out of debt that bad. I was willing to do just about anything to propel my journey forward. I'm one of those people that is either all in or not in at all. When I commit to something, it's all or nothing. I don't expect you to be as intense, but if you decide to be, your debt will be gone sooner.

I also went almost ten years without getting a new cell phone. I stuck with the old one for a long time, not wanting to increase my expenses. I kept the furnace low in the winter and didn't use an air conditioner in the summer. I limited where I traveled to save gas in my car. I stopped going out on the weekends. Instead, I started loving Saturday nights with the Suze Orman show on CNBC, which sadly is no longer on.

I had gone from buying anything I wanted to watching every dollar. I realized I couldn't afford the life I had been living and now had to make hard choices to clean up my mess. You're likely going to feel this way too. You'll see lowering your expenses as sacrifice and question whether it's worth it.

However, I challenge you to adjust your perspective. Instead of focusing on *sacrifice*, focus on *progress*.

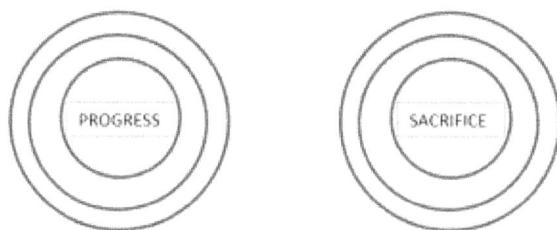

You get to choose. You can see reduced spending as sacrifice, or you can see it as progress to your goal. These two perspectives make all the difference.

It may feel hard, but at least you have the choice today. You get to decide what you will spend less on. You are in control right now. On the other hand, if you keep avoiding your spending problem, one day you won't have the luxury of creating your own plan. You'll end up bankrupt or worse, in retirement age but not able to retire because you have no money.

Some of these changes may be true sacrifices, but some changes are life improvements. My decision to stop going out on the weekends not only saved me money, but also lowered my alcohol consumption.

This journey really is a well-rounded life improvement journey. Your mental and physical health will likely soar during this journey as you are reshaping your life in a great way. Don't see going lean as negative. See it as a step in the right direction for your future self.

Myth 7: You Can Out Earn Your Crazy Spending

You're never going to earn enough to compensate for your frivolous spending.

The old me, the person who was in debt with no plan to get out, knew my career was heading in the right direction. At some point my growing income would hit the level of my spending, right? That's what I believed, and that's why I wasn't worried about my escalating debt in my late twenties. I was doing well at work and assumed my salary would keep climbing.

How wrong was I?

As I made more money, my debt actually got worse. I spent more, not only buying more, but buying more expensive items. I accumulated more student loans for my MBA. I ate out just about every meal. I was so focused on performing well at work and completing my MBA that I didn't give my money any time at all. I just kept spending without regard to the growing debt balances.

One of the oldest pieces of money advice is to spend less than you make. It is such common sense. When you think about it, of course, we should all spend less than we earn. But why does this advice slip our minds? Why don't we listen to it?

We have so many short-term desires which we're focused on, and in many cases, money isn't in the primary spot. Of course, many of us want to be wealthy, but accumulating wealth takes time, and we have higher priorities right now. Accumulating wealth is the path less taken. It's the path of discipline, consistency, and patience.

In today's society, we don't have to be patient to get that new car. Sign on the dotted line, and you can drive it home today. Instant gratification gets the best of us.

Who chooses long-term patience and discipline over fancy cars and houses today? Look at the number of likes on social media posts of pictures of high-end lifestyles versus posts about the actions required to create wealth. People want shiny objects, but don't want to put in the work to earn them.

When you truly understand how powerful it is to spend less than you make, your perspective changes. You'll happily curb your spending if it means you can invest extra this month or put more away for that investment property you've been saving for. When your financial goals become your priority, no matter how long they take, watch out. You are ready for major financial growth.

Excuses Create Destructive Cycles

You own your life. Things happen out of your control, but you own your reaction to those experiences. Take responsibility for the choices you've made. Take responsibility for where you are right now. Vow to yourself you will no longer play the role of victim or use excuses. Make this promise daily to yourself until it becomes a natural part of your thinking.

Excuses provoke feelings of being the victim and allow your mind to concentrate on all the negative reasons you can't do something. Once you aren't leaning on excuses in your mind, you'll have more capacity for productive thoughts and planning versus wasting your precious thoughts on justifying to yourself why you can't do something. You can move forward with a fresh perspective instead of constantly bringing yourself back to the same excuses.

Here are some examples:

- I have kids.
- I grew up poor.
- I'm not smart enough.
- People like me don't go far.
- I wasn't born with a silver spoon.

These are actual excuses I see in my X (formerly Twitter) comments all the time. It's easier to assume I was born rich, or I married rich, or I inherited my assets. In some ways I feel bad for these individuals because this is the foundation of their beliefs. These excuses are facts to them. They really don't believe they can take control of their money or become financially free. They can't even see the possibility of that.

Filling your mind with excuses of why you can't do something is like driving into a roundabout and never leaving. You don't accomplish anything. You just go in circles. Instead of driving in this vicious cycle, exit the roundabout, eliminate your excuses, and move forward toward your destination.

Bad things happen to everyone. It's our reaction that dictates how much we allow those negative events to sidetrack us. Successful people don't fall back to excuses. They acknowledge the bad event, and they figure out a way to move on. By forgetting your excuses and taking responsibility for where you are right now, you'll move outside of mediocrity and into the successful range. You'll get control of your money.

Let's exit the roundabout and never come back.

Tracking is Your Superpower

I've mentioned tracking your debt and spending a few times. I've emphasized this because tracking my money was the driver behind me going from $260,000 debt to millionaire. I know it doesn't seem like a powerful tool, but the act of writing down or typing into a spreadsheet your money is one of the most effective actions you can take. Tracking does so much for you.

First, we tend to anchor our minds to a number. If you've ever been part of a negotiation, you may have wanted to say the first number to anchor the other party to a number or you may take a different approach, but we get numbers stuck in our minds.

Many of us, including me, anchored our highest investment balance prior to this bear market, and now compare where we are to where we were. That high number is anchored in our minds. You may have an anchored weight in your mind. Maybe you were 20 pounds lighter in your twenties, and now you always compare your current weight to where you were. We all do this in many areas of our lives.

As we go through the month, making one-off purchases, we anchor that last purchase in our heads, but many of us don't accumulate the total of all our purchases. Instead, we only think about the last purchase or a big purchase in the month.

This anchoring effect doesn't let us see the whole picture until we actually write it down. It's amazing how surprised you'll be at how much you spend in one month when you start tracking.

Second, we only get so many thoughts per day, and when you intentionally focus your thoughts on tracking your money, those thoughts are powerful. Instead of being in the dark filled with uncertainty, you have the numbers in front of you. You approach your money completely differently, as you now see exactly what you have and how much you spend.

Instead of portraying negative thoughts on your money, you now approach it with determination and confidence. These emotions are much more powerful, and those emotions translate to your money.

And lastly, tracking gives you the power to make better decisions. It becomes clear which behaviors have positive results and which have negative results. You'll see the patterns of which behaviors push you forward and which behaviors hold you back.

You've put yourself back in the driver's seat where you can choose to accelerate or slow down when it's necessary. You are in control. You make the decisions. With this level of knowledge, you naturally start making better decisions.

Of course, you can take a vacation or go to a concert, but you're making that decision knowing that those choices will delay your debt pay-off. When you track your money, you know the outcome of your decision. Being in the know versus being in the dark is a game changer.

Eliminate Unnecessary Expenses

Eliminating unnecessary expenses doesn't mean sacrificing everything. It means prioritizing. You have different desires when it comes to your spending – true needs, high-priority wants, and low-priority wants. Your true needs include the basics to survive – rent, utilities, transportation, food. High priority wants could be restaurants you like, movie subscriptions you really enjoy, or boat expenses for your weekend excursions. They are anything you feel strongly about. Low priority spending could be a gym membership you only use once a month, clothes you keep buying but never wear, or furniture you don't need.

When you take the time to categorize your past spending, you are in for a surprise. You might realize you are spending a lot on low priorities and maybe not so much on things you thought were high priorities. By tracking every dollar, you will get more insight into your own behaviors. Maybe you think you're just a social drinker, but you're actually spending $250 a month on alcohol.

My brother is on top of his spending. A couple years ago he sent me a spreadsheet that listed his major spending categories for the year. He had literally tracked every dollar he spent that year. It was amazing. He didn't use a fancy app or website; he manually tracked it in a spreadsheet. He said this gave him so much clarity into his spending. He used this information to create spending goals for the following year, cutting in some areas and being more generous in others.

After you see what you're spending on, you become more aware of the unnecessary expenses and can take action. For example, are your children getting new toys every time you go to the grocery store, because it helps you get through your grocery shopping experience more peacefully? Maybe you're spending $200 on toys every month and didn't even realize it. The solution might be to go grocery shopping without your kids or to start saying no.

There are other expenses and fees that are completely unnecessary. Do you have auto-withdrawals for memberships you no longer use? It's time to cancel those. Do you have unexplained cash withdrawals from the ATM where you have no idea what happened to that cash? It's time to stop that.

Look at how many overdraft fees and late fees you are paying. These are unnecessary expenses that add up quickly and take away your hard-earned cash. Fees, although each one might seem small, add up fast. Paying fees is literally throwing away your money. You worked hard for this money, respect it and don't throw it away.

While I was working at the bank, I worked with a customer who was notoriously late on every payment. Her husband was serving in the military on active duty at this time. She received a huge direct deposit every month and literally within two days, she had blown most of it at Walmart. She was dealing with more than just money problems as I'm sure it was difficult to not have her husband home, but shopping wasn't the answer. Because of her shopping sprees, she ran out of money quickly and never had money to pay her bills. She averaged around $75 every month for late fees that she could have clearly paid on time.

I know limiting your spending changes you. Limiting my spending meant less nights out with friends. It meant I stayed home more and found free things to do, like walking and bike riding. This wasn't a negative, but my friends didn't necessarily want to change with me.

When we make these tough decisions, it is difficult. We are intentionally being different because we have a higher purpose. It's going to be hard, especially in the beginning. You're changing your habits.

You'll feel like your friends are continuing to have fun while you are sacrificing. This is completely normal. It gets better though. As you see progress and make this a game, you will feel better emotionally too. And, eventually, you will feel awesome for being able to put yourself through those discomforts when others didn't.

Increasing Your Credit Score

I briefly mentioned one advantage to having a good credit score in the last chapter. With great credit comes opportunities like zero-percent credit cards. As you saw, these can save you a lot of money.

A credit score doesn't tell you if someone is wealthy or not though. It doesn't tell you how much money a person makes or how much money a person invests. It only tells you how much debt someone has and how well that person manages their debt.

Let me repeat, a perfect credit score does not equate to wealth or high income. I think this is a huge misconception among many people.

A good credit score does, in fact, help lower some of your expenses. Let's get as lean as we can without significantly cramping our style. Let's reduce expenses by increasing our credit score. Examples of expenses that can be reduced are insurance on your house and vehicles, interest rates on your debt, and rent on your apartment.

People correlate a high credit score with less risk. When a lender, an insurance company, or a property management company sees a high credit score, they see someone who is more likely to pay their bills on time. They see someone who is more responsible and will not break their contract. This is why your credit score is so important. It's a score that doesn't show wealth, but it does illustrate some values, like responsibility.

You can access your credit score on many different websites. The government offers free access to check your credit history once a year from the three major credit companies, Equifax, Experian, and TransUnion. If you haven't checked your credit lately, go to www.annualcreditreport.com[1] and check your credit. This site will not provide your credit score for free, but they will show you all your open accounts and your payment history for free. You can look up Equifax, Experian, and TransUnion every year. Take advantage of this service. It's free, and you will gain insight into what the bank sees when they pull your credit. You'll know if you have any late payments in your history or any old collections holding you back. And, more importantly, you can compare the open accounts on your credit report to your debt tracker to confirm you've included all your open accounts.

---

1. http://www.annualcreditreport.com

How do you increase your credit score? Each of the three companies has its own calculation to determine your credit score. Credit scores range from 300 to 850. Any score above 720 is usually considered good credit. Even though we don't know the exact algorithm each company uses, we do know the main contributing factors for determining your score.

- **Late Payments**

If you're late more than 30 days on a payment, your credit score will be damaged. This should be a given, but when money is tight and you need to prioritize one payment over another, you may want to consider which one would hurt your credit more. For example, if you are over 30 days late on a utility, you will likely not get a ding on your credit report, however, the utility company may shut off your power. If you are more than 30 days late on a loan payment or credit card bill, this will be reflected on your credit report. There are risks and consequences to paying both late, but based on your circumstances, decide which is worse for you.

Your on-time payment history makes up almost one-third of your total credit score. If you haven't made your payments a priority in the past, make them a priority now.

- **Inquiries**

When you apply for loans at multiple banks or dealerships, the number of inquiries on your credit report increases. Although a couple inquiries do not hurt much, accumulating more than two impacts your score negatively.

Banks generally only inquire or pull someone's credit report when they have applied for a loan. If you're applying for loans with multiple companies, it's a sign you're either taking out a lot of loans or you're not being approved.

If you are getting multiple loans at the same time, the lenders will not be able to see your new debt payments. It usually takes at least 30 days for a new loan to show up on your credit report. Without seeing your whole picture, it's more difficult for them to make a good decision.

- **Age of Accounts**

As I was being trained to be a loan officer, I sat in a meeting with another loan officer and his customers. When the customers left, he pulled their credit report. Their credit score was decent, around 670. However, the age of all their credit card accounts was less than two years old. With my limited banking knowledge, I expected this couple to be approved. However, my colleague pointed out that this couple had likely gone through bankruptcy and the seven years had just recently passed because it was no longer showing up on their credit report. He knew that from the age of their accounts. These customers were in their fifties, but all their accounts were less than two years old. When you file for bankruptcy, there is a period of time when it isn't possible to open new credit. Many of your accounts are closed during this time, leaving you no opportunity for credit in the short term.

I have one credit card that I've had forever. This is the only card I use and the only account that shows up on my credit report as open. Because of its age and my good payment history, I've got a great credit score.

- **Credit Line Utilization**

Your score dramatically changes based on how much of your credit lines you have spent. This is much more important than I initially realized. As I paid down my debt, I checked my credit score every month since this was a free service from one of my credit cards. In one month, my credit card balances were 53% of my total credit limit because I was using the zero-percent credit card deals. The next month they were 29%. I thought my score would improve moderately due to this change, but my score grew over 40 points. This ratio is evidently very sensitive and will be impacted greatly by a small change.

I remember working with a potential loan applicant who had a horrible score, somewhere around the 450 range. She had a few older collections in her report, but she also had a balance of $299 outstanding on her only credit card, which had a limit of $300. Even though the value was relatively small, this ratio was so high that it significantly decreased her score. That was one example that surprised me. She only had $299 of total credit card debt. But, because her total credit limit was $300, she was using 99% of her total credit, which completely destroyed her score.

To minimize negative impacts to your credit score, try to keep your total credit card balances below 33% of your total credit limit. If you can do this, you will maximize your score.

- **History of Collections or Bankruptcy**

Many people think they can get out of their money problems by filing bankruptcy. The problem is there are consequences. Yes, there are situations where bankruptcy is necessary, but there are also situations where individuals think bankruptcy is the only answer and file it on a whim. I heard the other day that someone filed for bankruptcy with an overdue cable bill of about $200 and a credit card balance of around $9,000. That seems crazy to me. Filing for bankruptcy can cost thousands of dollars. Why spend thousands of dollars filing when your total debt is under $10,000?

Bankruptcy and collection agency activity shows up on your credit report and stays there for a long time. The consequences of bankruptcy are a reduced credit score, lower credibility with future banks, and higher all-around costs.

Maximize your credit score to lower your overall expenses. This is one of the easier ways to lower your overall expenses.

Action 7 – Calculate Your Net Worth

Now that you've created a budget and listed your total debts, the big question is: what is your net worth?

You've already done most of the work by listing your debts. The only remaining action is to add your assets.

These are your checking, savings, retirement, and other deposit account balances as well as the value of any real estate you own. These can be CD's (certificate of deposits), bonds, rental properties, primary residences, IRA's (individual retirement accounts), 401k's, pensions, 403b's. You can also add vehicles but know their value will continue to decline over time.

Next, subtract your total debts from your total assets. This is your net worth.

This can be scary. The first time I ever did this, my net worth was negative $83,423. It made me realize I had a lot of work to do.

If it's worse than you thought, don't give up. The fact that you took the time to write it down shows you are willing to learn and willing to change how you interact with money. The sooner you do this, the better.

Remember, don't confuse your net worth with your self-worth. Maybe your number is negative. Maybe you made choices that weren't the best. We all have. The great thing is that you recognize you made those choices. You recognize you are the key. You created this, and only you can clean it up.

Once you understand the power you have in your life, you can move forward. You don't have to avoid it any longer. You don't have to stay stuck. You can make changes today.

A negative net worth can only exist when we've taken on regressive debt and when we've spent more than we make. This is why it's important to avoid regressive debt and to pay it off as quickly as possible. Regressive debt takes you backwards, literally. It creates the ability for your net worth to be negative.

When you charge random things on credit cards and take out loans for vehicles that depreciate, you are left with a lot of debt and very little assets.

Here was the whole picture of my net worth from the last illustration of the debt only. My net worth was still negative, but I had made a huge improvement from the low point of the negative $99,000 it was. Now, I was sitting at negative $48,000.

Assets	Value	Debts	Balance	Monthly	Interest Rate	Annual Interest
		Credit Card 1	$2,957	$100	15.00%	$ 444
Checking	$600	Credit Card 2	$17,920	$397	0.00%	$ -
Savings	$100	Credit Card 3	$5,382	$100	0.00%	$ -
Total Cash	**$700**	Credit Card 4	$8,300	$100	0.00%	$ -
		Residence Mortgage	$62,366	$448	3.25%	$ 2,027
		Vehicle Loan	$8,619	$307	4.99%	$ 430
401k	$42,844	Student Loan 1	$29,532	$160	2.63%	$ 775
Jeep	$10,000	Student Loan 2	$0	$0	8.50%	$ -
Property	$75,000	Student Loan 3	$21,623	$156	6.80%	$ 1,470
		Student Loan 4	$20,138	$156	6.80%	$ 1,369
Total Assets	**$128,544**	**Total Debt**	**$176,837**	**$1,924**		**$ 6,515**
Net worth	**($48,293)**					

Seeing the progress from where I started with $260,000 debt and $16,000 annual interest to $177,000 debt and $6,500 annual interest was huge. However, seeing my net worth go from negative $99,000 to negative $62,000 to negative $48,000 was inspiring. Of course, I had the big goal to get out of debt, but I was also striving to get my net worth positive. Using this tracker was perfect for me as it illustrated my progress each month.

A year later I achieved that huge milestone when my net worth increased above zero. This is when I shifted up a gear. I saw the results and realized I could knock out this debt. I paid off over $30,000 in year two, and at the same time, my investments grew. The below table is one year later than the above table.

Assets	Value	Debts	Balance	Monthly	Interest Rate	Annual Interest
HSA	$952	Credit Card 1	$4,700	$86	15.00%	$ 705
Checking	$560	Credit Card 2	$19,307	$100	0.00%	$ -
Savings	$300	Credit Card 3	$6,800	$100	0.00%	$ -
Total Cash	$1,812	Credit Card 4	$2,000	$100	0.00%	$ -
		Residence Mortgage	$58,967	$448	3.25%	$ 1,916
401k	$68,032	Vehicle Loan	$5,299	$307	4.99%	$ 264
Jeep	$8,000	Student Loan 1	$28,838	$160	2.63%	$ 757
Property	$77,000	Student Loan 4	$20,049	$156	6.80%	$ 1,363
Total Assets	$154,844	Total Debt	$145,960	$1,457		$ 5,006
Net worth	$8,884					

I know this may not be as exciting for you, but you can do this too. That's what I want you to get excited about. I didn't do anything extraordinary other than practice some discipline and patience.

Having a positive net worth was a goal of mine for years, and it finally came true. It was no longer a vision; it was reality. It took around two years to get to this point, but it was completely worth it. You can see

I still had a long way to go to pay off my debt, but that's okay. I had accomplished a milestone, and I celebrated it.

Section 3: Retirement Investing
Create Your Ideal Life

Shifting your mindset is the foundation, eliminating your regressive debt is your focus until it's gone, and investing in your retirement happens in the background. It doesn't require much of your focus. You are going to set it up once and not think about it until your regressive debt is gone.

Investing toward your retirement early is the best way to capture the power of compounding. Recall the compounding chart; time is the key to compounding. The earlier you start investing in your retirement, the more time is on your side. Take this example. One person starts investing $250 a month at age 30 while another person starts investing the same amount at age 40. Let's assume they both average a 10% return until they are 65 years old.

The first person contributes a total of $105,000, and her balance is $894,000 at age 65. The second person contributes a total of $75,000, but her account is only valued at $325,000 at age 65. Ten additional years resulted in $569,000 more dollars.

If the second person wanted to achieve the same balance as the first person at age 65, she would have to contribute $690 each month and would contribute $207,000 over the 25 years. At age 65, she would have $894,000 in her account. In other words, she would have to contribute almost double that of the first person just to catch up.

Do you see how important time is for compounding? If the second person wanted to catch up, she would contribute more than double the monthly payments of the first person ($250 vs $690), even though she is only missing 10 of the total 35 years of investing.

Although it is vital to rid yourself of regressive debt, you still want to optimize your retirement investing by contributing something. I contributed 10% while I still had regressive debt. This allowed me to accumulate almost $119,000 in my retirement account when I became debt-free.

When I paid off my regressive debt, I wasn't starting from scratch. I already had a six-figure retirement account. Believe me, that felt good.

Digging myself out of debt was hard. It was a long journey. Becoming debt-free was an amazing feeling, and having a six-figure retirement account was the icing on the cake.

When my last debt was paid off, I immediately increased my 401k contribution to 22%. Because I no longer had monthly debt payments, I had the extra money to invest more. Eliminating debt frees you up emotionally, financially, and mentally. It literally frees up money for extra investing, and it emotionally frees up the burden you feel from it.

8: You're Going to Stop Working Someday

It can be difficult to picture your retirement, especially if your finances are out of control. There are multiple people in my life that constantly say they are never retiring. They are good people. They are smart. However, they can't seem to get a handle on their finances. When they want something, they buy it. For them, and I believe for many others, retirement seems so far away that it's not worth thinking about. It's so far in the future and there's no certainty that they'll live that long.

We find safety in our beliefs. We believe what we see, and we're more apt to take action on something we see now instead of something we can't see well in the future.

It doesn't matter if you can see it or not though. You're going to get old. You're lucky if you stay healthy while you age. You may not be so lucky though. What if something happens to your health before you're eligible for Social Security and you need to live on disability for a decade? You're not going to bring home as much as you currently do. And most health conditions aren't covered by disability.

I was listening to a podcast the other day and heard this story. A question came in from a woman in her early fifties. Out of nowhere, her husband fainted. The doctors determined he had a heart condition and recommended he didn't work in a stressful position any longer. That condition was not covered by disability. Most jobs come with stress. Luckily, this couple was on top of their finances. They only had a couple months left to pay off their mortgage and had a sizable retirement account.

What if something like this happens to you? Can you financially take care of yourself if you had to take off an extended period of time from work? What if you were forced to choose between retiring early or potentially damaging your health to work?

None of us know what the future holds. Don't assume that you can work the rest of your life and ignore your money. You don't know how long you will be capable of working.

Myth 8: You Can Live Comfortably on Social Security

Social Security isn't enough.

The average monthly Social Security check seems to be between $1,000 and $2,000. Can you live on $1,500 a month?

If you have debt, the answer is no. Add up your $400 car payment, your $100 student loan payment, your $1,000 mortgage or rent, and your $100 credit card minimum payment. That's $1,600 without even considering food, utilities, and other needs. You can't live on $1,500 a month with debt. It's just not possible.

Food, utilities, health care, and transportation add up. If you add debt payments, it's almost impossible to spend less than $1,500 a month. Let's say you live in a low-cost area and pay off your debt before you retire. If you do this, there is a chance you can live off $1,500 a month, but you're cutting it too close. What happens when an appliance goes out? Or the rent or property taxes go up? One extra expense can blow up your entire budget. Then what? Do you charge it on a credit card? Do you get a part-time job?

If you think I'm wrong, prove it to me. Live on less than $1,500 next month. If you can do this, I'm impressed.

I know you can't see it yet, but retirement is right around the corner. Have you noticed the older you get, the faster time flies? In your twenties, you shrugged off retirement, because you were so young. You had your whole life ahead of you. You wanted to get serious in your thirties, but again, you were still young and growing in your career. You told yourself you will make the big money in your forties. The problem is you get to your forties and think the same thing, or you finally realize retirement is only 20-some years away. You've already worked 20 years in your career and have little to show for it. You're already halfway through your working years in your mid-forties. It's time to start.

It's crazy how quickly the years go by. Stop waiting for the right time to start contributing to retirement. The right time is right now.

What Does it Really Mean to Retire?

I remember over a decade ago sitting in my boss' office reminiscing about how we both wanted to retire early. I was in my late twenties at the time. When we talked about it, my mind always equated retirement with no stress and no work. This was fun to do. Visualizing the work-free, stress-free life was great.

A few years later I talked to my best friend about our retirement dreams. One of our frequent activities was bicycling. We would take the afternoon off and find a bike path and ride for miles. We would talk about what it would be like when we didn't have to work. Again, I equated retirement with not working and no stress.

During all these memories I was also drowning in debt. Who was I to believe that I could retire early?

I didn't let my debt deter me though. I still dreamed about it. Then, a few years ago as I surpassed many of my net worth milestones, I started thinking more seriously about how to retire early. Instead of seeing a high-level vision, I was doing calculations and thinking through more details.

I realized that having a bunch of cash in my forties didn't really mean I could retire that early. Health insurance is expensive! And then, when I really thought about retiring, I thought, *what am I going to do every day with a lot of time but with limited funds?* It would be great to have time to work out every day, to spend more time with family and friends, and to not be stressed with work, but is a tight retirement my ideal life?

I would gain a lot of time, but I would need to sacrifice my spending for the rest of my life. That life didn't seem appealing to me. That wasn't the original vision I had for retirement. Now that I was making real traction in my finances, I started adding these details to my vision and I didn't like what I saw.

I wanted freedom in all ways, not just freedom in time, but also freedom in travel and other activities. The whole reason I was working hard and saving so much money was to have a comfortable retirement, not a tight retirement.

As I get older, I have a new vision of retirement. I still see freedom, but I understand that traveling and other desires come with a cost.

I also realize that retirement still comes with stress. Life brings stress whether you are working, or you aren't. You won't have a job to worry about, but you will still have relationships and extracurricular activities.

Retirement doesn't equate to happiness either. Happiness doesn't come to us at a point in time or through a big accomplishment. If you think your retirement is the event that will trigger your happiness, you are going to be very disappointed. You've got to find your inner happiness today. Don't pin it on a certain date or activity. Yes, it is exciting to have the ability to retire, but that excitement doesn't last. True inner happiness does.

No matter where you are financially or how old you are, take a few moments to fantasize about your retirement. You can make your vision high level or detailed. The more detailed you get, the more value you'll get from this exercise.

Retirement Doesn't Mean Relaxation 24/7

There are a few things to consider when you retire. First, if your life becomes 24/7 relaxation, you're going to lose your purpose. The first few weeks will feel amazing. You don't have to wake up to an alarm clock. Your time isn't dictated by your job. You can do whatever you want whenever you want. However, after a month or so, if you haven't found hobbies or purpose in other areas, this new freedom is going to take its toll. You may find that you start watching five hours of television a day. You stop socializing. You sleep much more than you ever used to. All the people around you still go to work, leaving you on your own all the time.

Jobs provide a social structure for us. We may not love the people we work with, but they are people, and those relationships are good for us. When you retire, you won't have the built-in schedule to see these people. Someone I know who is currently retired told me what he misses most about working are the relationships. You know this is true. How many times has someone left a company and you intended to stay in touch with them, but you didn't really stay in touch? It happens all the time. When you retire, much of your social network goes away with it.

Jobs provide time structure in our lives too. You may not like to get up early, but you live on a schedule primarily dictated by your job. Many of us don't like the hours we work, me included, but that's part of our jobs. When you don't have to work eight to ten hours a day, what will you do with your time? If you say, I'm going to start exercising, but you currently don't exercise at all, then I hate to inform you, but you likely won't start exercising just because you have more time. You've got to build the habits today while you're working to maintain them in retirement. I started running every other day and doing yoga on the non-running days. I'm building habits for when I retire in the next few years.

Jobs provide our identity in many cases. What's one of the first things you ask when you meet someone new? What do you do? We all like to know what others do for a living. It's interesting to hear about what other professions people do. We spend most of our waking hours at our jobs. Of course, we tie our identity to our jobs. When you spend a lot of time focusing on one area, you identify with it. You might be a mom, a dad, a coach, a fitness guru, a nurse, a delivery person, a cook, a mechanic, a lawyer, a doctor, a dentist, an analyst, a CEO, etc. Your job is a big piece of your identity, whether you like it or not.

Jobs provide purpose and a sense of fulfillment. Although we may not realize it, our jobs give us purpose. Most of us want our companies to succeed. We want to do our jobs the best we can. Our jobs contribute to the overall success of the greater mission of the company. I know you don't feel like this every day, nor do I, but deep down we have a need to contribute. We need a purpose. We need to feel satisfaction in our work. Knowing that you are contributing to help your customers deep down does feel good. When you no longer have a job, where will your purpose come from? How will you feel fulfilled?

Many of us have taken for granted these feelings. We don't consciously see our job taking care of these feelings, but in many cases, when you stop working, if you haven't consciously looked inside yourself to understand your true purpose and what makes you fulfilled, retirement is going to be difficult.

For all the complaining we do about our jobs, it's funny how much value they really provide for us, and we don't even appreciate it until it's too late. Don't plan to become a vegetable in front of the television for your retirement. Find a purpose. Find a hobby. Find people. Find these before you take the plunge into retirement.

Your Money Needs Time to Grow

Now that you know retirement is coming, you have a vision, and you know Social Security isn't enough, you're ready to start investing in your retirement.

Recall from the compounding example, you aren't going to get wealthy by putting your money under a mattress. The majority of your retirement accounts will be made up of growth, not your contributions. The previous example showed at the end of 40 years, at an 8% return, your total account balance would be $1,678,000, but you would have only contributed $240,000. That means the growth would be $1,438,000 of the account. In other words, 86% of your total retirement balance would be from growth.

Let's say you don't have 40 years until retirement; you only have 20 years. Put in the same $500 a month at an 8% return, and you'll have almost $300,000 in the account in 20 years. Of that $300,000, you'll only contribute $120,000. That means, again, the majority of the account is growth which is $180,000. In just 20 years, 60% of your retirement balance is growth alone. Are you starting to see how important compounding and time is? The longer you invest, the more growth you'll have. This is why it's so important to start today.

This is one reason why many financial experts tell you to never withdraw or take a loan from your retirement. Sure, the account representatives describe that taking a loan doesn't hurt you, but you are missing vital years of growth via compounding. I bet they never mention this.

I made this mistake. In 2011 I closed my 401k from my previous employer. The balance was around $29,000. Now, I didn't end up with

$29,000 when I withdrew it. Instead, I was hit with a 10% penalty and taxes on it. I believe I netted around $23,000. I lost $6,000 immediately. I don't know if you remember 2011, but we were still recovering from the 2008-2009 housing crisis and the market was low. That $29,000 would be worth well over $100,000 today if I hadn't touched it just twelve years ago.

That's how we learn though. We make mistakes. I hope you don't make this mistake. Don't allow your hard-earned retirement money to be penalized. Don't stop the compounding that is taking place. Let it grow until you're old enough to withdraw it penalty-free.

Tax Treatment of Retirement Accounts

Retirement investing offers many perks. Of course, the primary perk is that you will have funds to retire, but a very close second perk is the tax benefits that come with these accounts.

Why pay the government more than you need to? Instead, take advantage of tax benefits, no matter which type of retirement account you choose.

You have the choice to save taxes today or in the future based on the type of account you choose to contribute to. If you decide to save in the future, you will save much more in the long run.

Roth (Post-tax, After-tax)

I'm sure you've heard of a Roth IRA or Roth 401K, or even a post-tax 401K. When you contribute to a Roth account, you contribute dollars that have already been taxed, post-tax dollars.

Let's say your paycheck gross amount is $2,000, but after taxes and insurance, you take home $1,200. For a Roth account, you would be contributing money from that $1,200. This money has already been taxed. Your total taxable income is still $2,000. Contributing to a Roth account doesn't give you tax benefits in the year you contribute to it.

However, **Roth accounts give you the most tax benefits overall** because you do not pay any taxes on the growth. Let's say you contribute $150,000 over the next 25 years into your Roth account. This $150,000 has now grown to $475,000 due to compounding. In other words, you've had $325,000 of growth in the account. When you withdraw these funds from your contributions and your growth, you don't have to pay any taxes.

The more your account grows, the more tax savings you'll experience in a Roth account. This is what makes the Roth accounts so appealing. You will save so much in taxes by paying the tax today. Remember, growth will make up the vast majority of your account balances in the future. All growth is tax-free in a Roth account.

Traditional (Pre-tax, Before tax)

The Traditional is the most common type of retirement account, simply because it's existed longer than the Roth. The Traditional account allows you to get the tax benefit in the year you contribute to the account. In our prior example, if your paycheck was $2,000 and you contributed $500 to a Traditional account, then this $500 comes off your gross value before taxes are calculated.

In other words, you would only be taxed for receiving $1,500 on that paycheck. The immediate tax benefit is really appealing to people. I get it. You want the tax advantage as soon as you can get it. You're making a choice between yourself today and your future self.

The problem with the Traditional account is when you're retired, you're going to pay a lot more in taxes. Let's look at the same example as above. You contribute $150,000 over the next 25 years, and your account has grown to $475,000, so again, you have $325,000 in growth.

When you start withdrawing from this account, you'll pay taxes on every withdrawal. That means, you'll pay taxes on the $150,000 that you previously received the tax benefit on and on the $325,000 growth. When you're retired, taxes are the last thing you want to think about.

Many people argue that they are in a higher tax bracket while they're working. Why wouldn't they take the tax savings now instead of waiting until they're in a lower tax bracket.

What they don't realize, however, is the comparison isn't apples to apples. You can't compare being taxed on $150,000 in both scenarios. $150,000 is the right number for the Roth in this example, but you'll be taxed on $475,000 for the Traditional. This is the difference I see many people not taking into consideration when they make this comparison.

Let's do the real math.

This table shows the difference for this specific example. If you were to contribute $500 a month to a Roth and Traditional for 25 years and average an 8% return, you would pay far less taxes on the Roth over your lifetime. Even if your tax bracket does fall, it would take a significant tax bracket change to come out even.

Roth Total Tax Paid		Traditional Total Tax Paid	
Tax on $150K (during working yrs)		Tax on $475K (during retirement yrs)	
Tax Percentage	Tax Paid	Tax Percentage	Tax Paid
25%	37,500	25%	118,750
20%	30,000	20%	95,000
15%	22,500	15%	71,250
10%	15,000	10%	47,500
7%	10,500	7%	33,250
5%	7,500	5%	23,750

This table says if you were in the 25% tax bracket during your working years, you would need to fall into the 7% tax bracket in order to make the Traditional an equitable choice ($37,500 versus $33,250 in taxes paid). If you were in the 15% tax bracket during your working years, you would have to fall to below the 5% tax bracket in order for the Traditional to be an equitable choice. ($22,500 versus $23,750)

These are just the tax ramifications of the Roth versus the Traditional. The Roth has other conveniences as well, but we won't dive into much of the detail here. There are income restrictions on the Roth accounts though. Consult your tax professional for more details.

If you have the option to contribute to a Roth 401K at your job, this is the highly recommended choice. Also, take advantage of the Roth IRA. Within certain income limits, almost anyone can open a Roth IRA.

Action 8 – Invest in Your Retirement

Although the Retirement Investing stage appears to be third, it occurs simultaneously with paying off your regressive debt and improving your mindset. When you're ready to get serious about your money, it's time to start investing in your retirement.

Stop missing out on your employer's contribution. Many companies offer to match their employees' contributions up to a certain percentage.

The minimum you should contribute depends on your employer. Make sure you are contributing at least enough to receive the full match. Every company is different. To get the full match you will likely need to contribute between 3% and 15% of your paycheck to your retirement account, usually a 401k or 403b. Set this up early and ensure the contributions are automated. You don't want to think about these contributions. Once it's set up, the less you think about it during your regressive debt pay-off, the better.

There are different types of retirement accounts. If your employer offers a match, then getting the match is priority number one. Companies are required to use a Traditional account for the match. If your company offers both the Traditional and Roth accounts, then prioritize the Roth first. As you just saw, the tax savings over your lifetime will be much higher in the Roth account.

During my debt-payoff phase, I contributed 10% toward retirement. This gave me a nice balance when I became debt-free. You choose how much you want to contribute. My suggestion is to contribute between 8% and 15%, or at least enough to get the full company match.

Again, you are going to set this percentage and forget it until all your regressive debt is paid off. I don't want your focus to be on this retirement account. I want your full focus to be on paying off your regressive debt.

You'll likely have a few investment options to choose from when opening your retirement account. Depending on the options in your account, choose growth stock low-cost mutual funds or index funds. I personally don't like buying too much of my own company's stock. If you do this, you're putting a lot of eggs in one basket. What if your company goes side-ways? You might lose your job, and their stock price may tank. That's a double whammy you want to avoid.

I would also avoid the time-defined investments. These are investments usually titled "2045" or "2055". As you get closer to retirement, these funds tend to invest more of your money into bonds and other less risky areas. In other words, your return will be lower. These also come with higher fees and aren't worth it.

Instead, look up the expense ratios of the investment options. Find one that mimics one of the major stock indexes (S&P 500, Nasdaq, Dow Jones) with a low expense ratio (less than 0.25%). This will limit your fees, and historically has provided good growth over time.

Today

As you've seen in these compounding examples, compounding takes time. It takes time to build your contributions to the point where the growth takes over and momentum takes hold.

No matter how old you are right now, it's not too late to start, but you do need to start.

Compounding gets more powerful as you give it more time to work. You saw in the prior chart that at the beginning, compounding doesn't make much difference. The line was similar to linear results. However, after time and balances increase, the power of compounding really takes off.

At my first job out of school, my starting salary was $22,500. After the first year they raised it to $25,000. My manager emphasized how large the raise was in percentage terms, over 10%. I wasn't impressed. Of course, a 10% raise is awesome, but when you're barely making minimum wage after graduating with student loans, it wasn't that exciting to me. I kept thinking, if I had a salary of $50,000 or $100,000, that 10% would be something. 10% of $50,000 is $5,000, and 10% of $100,000 is $10,000.

It's very similar in compounding. The bigger the balance you accumulate, the more powerful that 8% return is. If you have $10,000 in your retirement account and make an 8% return, you've made $800. If you have $100,000 in your retirement account and make an 8% return, you've just made $8,000. That's a lot of money. Sometimes we emphasize the percentage growth more than the absolute growth, but the absolute growth, $8,000, is what we're using to determine whether we have enough money to retire. It's that absolute number that gives us an idea of how much we can expect to live on.

This is why starting today is so important. The earlier you start, the more you can accumulate, and the more powerful compounding becomes.

9: Stick with Simplicity

Have you ever noticed the simple choice is almost always the right answer? When we complicate things, such as investing in things we don't understand or borrowing to invest, the outcome is always worse.

I'm finally realizing how awesome the simplest things in life are. Before I got serious about my money, I had multiple deposit accounts at different banks and lots of credit cards. I was trying to keep my money compartmentalized, thinking I was keeping it organized, but in reality, I had little balances everywhere, and wasn't keeping track of them well. Today, I have one checking account, one credit card, and a few investment accounts. I have simplified my money as much as possible.

We choose simple over complex naturally in the non-financial areas of our lives. When you get a new email, do you prefer to read the simple, clear, concise email, or the long, bulky complicated one? Of course, you choose the simple one. If it's too hard to read, it's probably not worth your time. Apple is well known for its simple packaging and its intuitive operating system. It's simple for us. We can learn it easily. We're drawn to simple and intuitive in many aspects of our lives, but for some reason we want to over-complicate our money. We choose the most complicated credit options because they seem sophisticated.

You might have 12 credit cards, because one gives you the most points at gas stations, one gives you the most points at their store, one gives you points for your next flight, and one doesn't have an annual fee. You spend so much time and energy in this complicated web of credit that doesn't really provide much extra money. If you consider the amount of time you spend on this, are you really getting any benefit at all?

This is the same on the investment side. Instead of just picking an index fund or a cheap mutual fund with a history of growth, you come up with a mix of mutual funds, stocks, and bonds. You look into options and derivatives. You leverage your accounts. You buy and sell quickly before the market has time to grow. Or you pick the financial advisor that sounds smart because he doesn't use everyday language. The more complex he makes it sound, the more you want in.

It's so easy to get sucked into these complicated credit card schemes and investing strategies because they sound cool. They might sound sophisticated, like you really know what you're doing with your money. But, in reality these over-complications are just consuming your time and your focus. You're focusing on the wrong things.

Go the simple route. Decide that debt is not your friend and investing doesn't have to be complicated. You can buy index funds and reap the rewards of compounding. You don't need to spend much time on it. You don't have to use every bit of energy on your strategy.

Myth 9: Get-Rich-Quick Schemes Make You Rich

If it sounds too good to be true, then you're not getting the truth.

Get-rich-quick schemes are all around us, masked in a variety of facades, such as the newest crypto-currency coin that's going to be the one, the strategy on social media that will earn you $10,000 a month, or the stock investing method that will make you a millionaire in a year.

It's easy to get sucked into these schemes, especially if you believe the results these people are promising. However, people selling get-rich schemes are the ones who get rich. Don't fall for these breath-taking results. Real wealth takes time. You will save yourself a lot of time, money, pain, and hassle if you accept these sales pitches as schemes.

I heard this story from a caller on a podcast a few years ago. A caller's husband was working in a different state. He wanted to be closer to his wife, so he took a job closer to their home with a pay cut. To make up for the lost income, they thought flipping houses would be a good option. They decided to go to a seminar, and $70,000 later they had not yet purchased a property. They accumulated $70,000 in debt from this real estate seminar and had nothing to show for it. The company told them they were invited to the 'next level' which they were excited about. They were so caught up in the words these individuals were saying that they got off track of their original purpose. When beginning in real estate flipping, there is very little information that is worth $70,000. The concept of flipping real estate is simple. Find a cheap house in a nice neighborhood that can be renovated and sell it for a profit. Obviously, there is a bit more to it than this, but these details can be learned through books or talking to other flippers, contractors, and real estate agents.

I thought I was going to get rich with penny stocks in my early twenties. I had $2,000 and deposited it into an account where I could buy penny stocks. At first, I got lucky. My $2,000 went up to $4,300. I should have cashed out right then, but I didn't. Then, just a few days later, my $2,000 was down to $500. The stock plummeted. What I learned was people had bought this stock for pennies and then promoted it like crazy on the Internet. The publicity created a price bubble, increasing the stock price significantly. That's when these people behind the scenes sold their shares and took their profit, leaving me and many others with a valueless stock. I held onto that stock for a few years before I finally sold it for less than $10.

If something sounds too good to be true, then it most likely is too good to be true. Don't get caught up in the pictures other people are painting for you. Stop and analyze what you are doing. Is it simple or complicated? Do you fully understand it? If you don't understand it, then it's most likely a trick to take your money.

Instead of trying to get rich quick, create a long-term plan and stick with it. Consistency and simplicity are the keys to real wealth building. There are no complicated short-cuts.

Complexity is Tempting

Aren't we all a little tempted by complexity? When you hear someone talking about the intricacies of the stock market or derivatives or crypto currency, it's very easy to be tempted into putting your money into these. Financial advisors, attorneys, and doctors are the most recognized as articulating simple concepts with overly complex language. They've been trained with this vocabulary, and they use it in many cases when it's not necessary.

These professions and others use their authority to give advice. The more complex they make the advice, the more their clients feel they need these people as advisors. Don't get caught up in their words. They may create complexity to build dependence on them.

When we create complexity in our lives, our relationships deteriorate, our time gets wasted, and our financials turn upside down. Complexity may sound appealing, but it takes more time. For example, think about a process you do at your job. Is the process too complex? Have you already thought of ways to do it quicker and better? There are so many things we do every day that are more difficult than they need to be. We may not even do this on purpose, but it happens.

I see this in my job all the time. There is one individual I've transferred work from multiple times. His processes are so complex when he trains me. His spreadsheets have 30 tabs in them. It's a nightmare to figure out exactly what he's doing. He tells me the time it takes him to do these processes. By the second time I've done these processes, I've condensed the spreadsheet down to 5 tabs and cut the time in half. It boggles my mind how complex he makes everything when there is a simple solution that would save so much time.

Some professions use complexity on purpose to create a buzz – that hot new product. The example I'm thinking of is reverse mortgages. Lenders convince older individuals who don't have much saved in retirement to take out a reverse mortgage. If you know anything about this product, you know this is a complicated product with lots of conditions. The individuals just see the benefits of having monthly cash flow in their pockets. They don't think of all the ways it can go wrong. For example, if the individual lives too long, their cash receipts will end. Not only will they no longer receive cash from the lender, but the lender could foreclose on their house. I thought the whole point of a reverse mortgage is to help the customer have a better retirement. Instead, the customer risks getting foreclosed on at the worst possible time in her life.

Complexity is not sophisticated. Complexity isn't authority. We need to stop being attracted to complicated things we don't fully understand. People who sell complexity know they have the upper hand. They create a vision of their product's benefits for you without telling you all the risks. Stop listening to these individuals. They only want to sell products. They aren't really going to help you improve your finances even though they are describing that vision.

Simplicity is always the best route to go. Stick with decisions and products where you fully understand them.

Simplicity can be the Path Less Taken

Don't mix up simplicity and complexity with easy and hard.

Simple doesn't mean easy. There are no shortcuts. This is where the get-rich-quick schemes trap us. The people selling these make it look so easy. They describe all the upside to their schemes and none of the downside. For example, a real estate seminar might emphasize the profit potential, the ease of finding the right properties, and the flexibility of the business, but they fail to mention the risk in overspending your budget, paying too much for a property, or the difficulty in finding the deals.

In this example, instead of paying for a seminar, be proactive. Offer to take another flipper to lunch to get tips, reach out to real estate agents, and read books on flipping. These are likely more difficult paths because you have to do the legwork. You've got to find the people to talk to and actually read the books. You've got to be proactive. It is more work, but if you really want to flip properties, it will be worth it, and you won't lose $70,000 on a real estate seminar.

This is just one example, but there are so many examples of us trying to find the easiest path even if it is more expensive. Instead of handing over your hard-earned money, figure out cheaper ways to do it. Find a free option if you can. The Internet is a vast resource of information if you just look.

Similarly, it's more difficult to sacrifice some of your income today to invest in retirement, but taking that hard path today makes your retirement much easier. The hard decision of sacrificing today doesn't mean it's not simple. It is simple and it's hard. The simplicity is that if you invest money today and consistently invest money into assets that appreciate like index funds, you will have a comfortable retirement. It's simple logic. You can understand this. However, the act of sacrificing that income today can be hard.

Shortcuts don't work. Simple can be hard. Take the simple, hard path anyway.

Prove You Can Handle a Little

Learning to manage what you have, even if it's just a little, is the way to grow your money. You might think a windfall would solve all your problems, but it doesn't work that way. You've got to show that you can manage what you have today. When you can manage a little well, only then are you ready to accumulate a lot.

When people inherit too much before they understand how to keep it and grow it, they blow through it quickly, being left with nothing. Take the example of lottery winners. Most lottery winners end up broke. They continue behaving in the same way they did prior to winning. They spend what they have, and more. In many cases, they end up in a worse position after the win. The money came too fast. They didn't have time to learn how to manage their money and how to save and invest their money. Again, money comes down to behavior. Remember, it's not math, because of our emotions. Start with a little money and grow it slowly. You'll have time to learn and make smaller mistakes which is much better than making larger mistakes with larger sums.

Don't keep believing your habits will change when you have more money. It's very similar to retirement. You might think you will exercise more when you have more time, but if you can't make time for exercising today, then you won't exercise when you're retired. If you can't keep money in your checking account today, then you won't be able to when you make more money. Your habits don't change with external circumstances. Your habits only change when you make the effort to change them.

My neighbor's barn burnt down a few years ago. It was devastating for that family. They lost a few horses in the fire. They ended up getting a large sum from the insurance company, nearly $100,000. They could have done many things with this money. They had roughly $100,000 balance left on their mortgage. They had car loans and credit card balances. Had I been in their shoes, I think I would have paid off the existing debt, but instead, they decided to rebuild the barn. Instead of just replacing the old barn, they upgraded. This new barn is bigger and has the most modern horse stalls. They also bought a new truck and have a loan on the truck. They no longer have any of this insurance money, and they still have a mortgage on their property. Last summer I heard them arguing, and I heard the words, "I can't afford it," come out of their mouths. They had so much money for a short period of time, but their behaviors didn't change, and today they are in a worse position than they were prior to receiving the $100,000. It just amazes me how people repetitively make bad decisions with their money, and they can't see it. I need to repeat that. They had a check for $100,000. Instead of making any good decisions with this money, they have a nice big barn for two horses, and they have a nice big truck with a truck loan.

If you don't take action today to improve your money habits and behaviors, no amount of money will help you. I want to explain this to my neighbors so badly. I keep seeing them make mistake after mistake.

This is why it's good to start small and grow your money slowly with your mindset. Accepting that you don't have much at the beginning is good. The sooner you understand how to manage a few dollars, the sooner you will receive more. If you don't take the time to learn how to manage what you've got because you think a small amount doesn't matter, then you will never win with money.

Building something great takes time. You've got to have the tortoise mentality, not the hare mentality. I'm sure you remember that old story from your childhood. The tortoise and the hare decide to race. Everyone, including the hare, knows that the hare is much faster than the slow tortoise. The hare is confident, so confident in fact that he gets distracted during the race, and the tortoise ends up winning. The longer I live, the more I see this truth every day. The consistent, persistent, and patient person is the person who succeeds. Great things really do take time. You must start small though.

Action 9 – Automate Where You Can

Technology is great in many ways. One of those ways is automation. Remember, simple is usually best. For example, most employers will automatically withdraw the designated amounts you've chosen from your paychecks and deposit them into your retirement accounts. You can also set up how much you want to go into each investment fund within those retirement accounts. Once you've set this up, you don't have to touch it again, especially while you are paying off regressive debt. These withdrawals automatically happen every paycheck. If you do this at the beginning of your career, you'll never miss this money.

If you decide to start contributing to your retirement today, you will see a slight drop in your paycheck value. Remember, you are doing this for your future self and for a better retirement. This small sacrifice is completely worth it.

If your employer doesn't offer a retirement-sponsored account like a 401k or 403b, you can set up an IRA with a discount brokerage. You can contribute up to $6,500 into an IRA if you're 49 years old or less. You can contribute up to $7,500 if you're at least 50 years old based on the 2023 contribution limits. Set up recurring withdrawals. Align the timing of the auto withdrawals to your paychecks.

Similarly, if you are self-employed, you can set up a Simplified Employee Pension (SEP) with a discount brokerage and automate as much as possible.

The more you automate your retirement contributions, the less you have to think about them. The less you think about them, the more focus you can devote to paying off your regressive debt.

Automate everywhere you can. Take advantage of our technology today, and don't get distracted with your retirement investing. This is a one-time set up while your primary focus is paying off your regressive debt.

10: Create Your Retirement Goal

We started thinking about our vision of retirement a couple chapters ago. This is the chapter where we define the details around that vision. This is where we create a plan, transforming that vision into a goal.

In order to create a goal, you need your 'why' and your 'what'. We'll come up with the 'what' in this chapter, but let's first take a few minutes to think about your 'why'.

Is your retirement vision spending time with your grandkids or volunteering at your favorite charities or sitting at the beach? Is your vision working on your hobbies or buying an RV and driving around the country? It doesn't matter what your 'why' is, but you've got to feel strongly about it. This purpose is the reason you will start loving to invest as much as you can today. This purpose will inspire you to create more income today in order to give you more time tomorrow.

Your purpose is something you are running toward. It's something you want to pursue. Don't let your purpose be something you are running from. Don't just look forward to not working. Don't run from your job. Run to something. Figure out what it is specifically that you're looking forward to in retirement. Of course, you will have a lot more time, but what are you going to do with all your extra time?

I have a list of things I'm going to do when I'm retired. These are things I'm partially doing today. When time frees up, I will become much more active in these pursuits. Remember, you are most likely not going to pick up a new hobby, habit, or interest just because you're retired. If your 'why' is to become physically fit and compete in races around the world, but you haven't run in years, I don't think extra time is going to give you the motivation to run. Make your vision of retirement realistic. In most cases, the activities you spend your time on today will get more of your time during retirement. Maybe you have a hobby that you want to turn into a business. Maybe you run today, just not as regularly as you'd like.

If you do have a goal in retirement, but can't seem to make time for it today, that's your challenge. Figure out how to create a few hours each week to squeeze in this activity now. If it's something that will be a priority during your retirement, you must make it a priority today to see if it's really something you want to pursue.

It's similar to when you were starting your career. You didn't know exactly what you wanted to do with your life, so you tried different jobs, you studied different fields, and you talked to people in different industries. You were feeling your way through until you found something that worked for you. It's very similar in retirement. Get your feelers out now for the priorities you believe you'll have in retirement. The sooner you do this, the more prepared you'll be and the more motivated you will be to contribute to your retirement accounts today.

Myth 10: Retirement Happens at a Certain Age

Retirement is a value not an age.

There are so many people I know that believe they are going to work until their sixties because they don't see another way. These are some of my closest friends and family. I want to tell them all the time that they can make a difference. The biggest tragedy is that because they don't see another way, they don't exert much extra effort into making more money or investing what they can today. Where there's no hope, there is also no try.

What makes this situation worse is that when they turn 62 or 65 or 67 and start to receive their Social Security checks, they'll realize that $1,500 a month isn't going to provide much security. The Social Security checks I saw while working at the bank were very small in many cases. Who wants to go from working for 40 years and then end up living on around $1,500 a month for their retirement? That doesn't seem like a relaxing way to spend my last years on this earth.

Instead of assuming Social Security is the solution, you must believe deep down it's not the answer.

In the prior section I mentioned we would determine your 'what' or your target for retirement. This is the value you need to have invested to retire comfortably. The great thing about this target is that you don't have to be 65 years old when you retire. You don't have to wait that long if you hit this number sooner.

These are the steps to determine what your target is.

1. Determine how much your monthly expenses will be.

When you start tracking every expenditure, you'll soon have a good idea of how much you spend each month. If you've only been tracking your expenses for a few months, remember there are quite a few expenses that only come up once or twice a year – annual gifts, property insurance, home and vehicle insurance, and one-off medical expenses. Also, don't forget to add money for additional costs in retirement, such as more travel and increased health insurance costs. For simplicity, let's assume your monthly expenses are planned at $4,000 per month.

Now, assuming your money is in Traditional accounts or taxable accounts, you'll also need to pay tax on the withdrawals (distributions) during retirement. Spending $4,000 per month means you need to withdraw at least $48,000 per year plus tax. Let's assume this level of income puts you in a 14% tax bracket. That equates to $6,700 for taxes, meaning you will need to withdraw a total of around $55,000 ($48,000 + $6,700) each year.

1. Determine how much passive income you must earn.

In this example you must have at least $55,000 per year to cover your expenses and taxes. You can earn passive income in many ways. Two popular ways are rental income from real estate and index funds.

If you have rental income, be conservative. What was your average net profit in the last few years? Let's say in this example, you earn $15,000 per year, and you are planning to keep these properties through your retirement.

Because of this rental income, you only need to come up with $40,000 each year ($55,000 less $15,000).

To determine how much you would need in an investment portfolio, use the 4% rule, also known as the Trinity Study, which originated from three professors at Trinity University. The 4% rule states you can withdraw 4% from your investment portfolio balance without much risk of running out of money. In other words, if your money is in investments averaging around an 8% return, then you can withdraw 4% of your total balance each year without consuming the entire balance over your lifetime. Most index funds average over 8%. As you know, there is volatility in the market. You won't make 8% every year. Some years you will lose 10% and other years you will make 19%, but it all averages out.

Let's return to the example of your net expenses after the rental income of $40,000. Divide your annual required income by 4% to come up with how much you need in your investment accounts. In this case, $40,000 divided by 4% is $1,000,000. In other words, you need $1,000,000 in your investment accounts to retire. That is your target. This is your retirement value.

You may be thinking, how am I ever going to save $1,000,000? Remember, this doesn't mean you have to contribute $1,000,000 into your investment accounts. Let compounding do the work for you. The vast majority of your retirement accounts will be made up of growth, not your contributions. This is why it's so important to start retirement investing sooner than later.

Determine the value you will contribute each paycheck and start investing today. Let compounding do the work for you. While you still have regressive debt, find a contribution amount that works for you. Maybe it's 6%, 8% or 10%. Just make sure it's enough to get 100% of your employer's match if they offer one.

Your Full-time Salary is the Cornerstone

When I first started this journey, I was making $78,000 gross salary at my full-time job. I had just started with a new company and was investing a lot of time into learning about the company, culture, and products. And I was finally getting serious about my own finances which was a huge step for me. At this point in my life, these were my two biggest commitments – my debt and my job.

Much research has shown that millionaires have multiple streams of income. Creating extra income is awesome, especially if it's passive income. However, depending on what phase of life you're in, don't discount your full-time salary. Your full-time salary provides you stability to get financially fit. Keep your full-time role a priority, no matter what goals you have outside of it. If you keep it a priority and continue growing your contribution to your company, your salary will grow. My salary grew greatly through the ten years of my debt-free journey.

I focused on strengthening my professional relationships, becoming an expert in certain areas, and buying into the mission of my company.

Although my long-term goal is to retire early, I want to maximize my time with my company. I don't discount anything they've done for me as I wouldn't be where I am today without them. If your full-time job isn't your passion, that's okay. You aren't alone. However, don't let that be the reason you limit your growth by displaying that attitude. That attitude won't get you promoted and won't increase your salary.

Go the extra mile and watch as it is paid back to you over time. If you feel like you've gone the extra mile for your company and haven't received much in return, it might be time to look for another company. All companies aren't built equal, and my experience might not be yours. I realized early on that one of the companies I worked for would never pay me what I'm worth, and I simply left. I wasn't mad. I didn't have a bad attitude. I just found a better company.

Let's face it, the majority of us are working in roles that are not our dream jobs. I'm included. I really like my company. I do my job well. I learn the latest tools, and I continue improving my efficiency. I enjoy a lot about my job. However, it's not my dream. I have a different calling. This doesn't mean I quit my full-time job and go after my dream full time. I still have bills to pay, and my calling is going to take time before it's profitable. I'm investing money today in myself to create the foundation for my next steppingstone. The only way I am funding this is because I am debt free, and I have the stability of my full-time paycheck.

When I worked at the bank, I got quite a few interesting requests. One was from a girl who I had known in high school. She came in ready to start her business – to sell make-up. I liked that she was inspired. The problem was she didn't have a full-time job. She wasn't making any income. She wanted to borrow money to buy her first batch of product. If you have no money coming in, how do you expect to make payments? I tried to explain this logic to her, but I don't think I was successful. You've got to have a foundational income to start investing in a side business.

Your full-time job is the key to investing in retirement and paying off your regressive debt. Don't discount your job. Instead, make the most of it and take advantage of it.

Action 10 – Make More Income

I know I just emphasized how important your full-time job is, and it is, but I also want to challenge you to earn more income. What can you do to bring in more money every month without compromising the value you give to your full-time job? There are many opportunities for part-time work. Driving down the street, there are endless Help Wanted signs. The labor market favors the employee right now. Companies are paying higher-than-average wages for retail and restaurant work.

If you need more flexibility in your hours or need to be at home, try working from home on a part-time gig. If you want to start your own business, there are plenty of opportunities online as well. You don't have geographic barriers when you work online. Opportunities to make money online are everywhere. Be creative when thinking about a side hustle. What skills could you offer? Could you start your own business? Can you work for someone else remotely? With COVID19, the world is a different place. You can easily make money from your home if you have an Internet connection. Even before COVID19, there were remote opportunities, but now they are everywhere.

Does your employer offer overtime? My brother-in-law is a nurse and due to the shortage of nurses, he was getting large daily bonuses for any days he worked above his three 12-hour shifts each week. If you're in an industry that has a labor shortage right now, take advantage of it. Employers are paying extra wages and bonuses just to get people to work. Think about your career trajectory. Do you have aspirations to grow within your company? Start adding more value. Get involved in projects. Learn outside your function.

Today is a great time to earn more income. The opportunities are abundant.

You have to want it though, and you have to be willing to work for it. I never said this would be easy.

Patience and Consistency are an Unstoppable Combination

Most big goals aren't accomplished overnight or in a week but through patient perseverance.

I have never been a patient person. The younger me didn't like waiting. I liked to get where I was going quickly, which is why I racked up quite a few speeding tickets in the past. Luckily, with age I've started to appreciate time differently. I understand that building something great takes time. In my youthful business exploits I never gave my ideas a chance to get off the ground. I was in too big of a hurry to find the one big hit. I jumped from idea to idea to try to get ahead. I never gave those ideas enough time to blossom.

It takes time to build something great. If you understand this from the beginning, you'll be less inclined to give up if the process takes longer than expected.

The majority of millionaires are millionaires because they consistently invested in their 401k accounts. Per the IRS website, in 2023 the individual contribution limit for a 401k is $22,500. You can't invest in your 401k for only five years and create a million dollars in your 401k. The contribution limits make this mathematically impossible. It takes time. Compounding and contributions over a few decades are the driver to turn that original $22,500 into a million dollars. There are no short cuts.

If you just contribute $300 a month starting at age 25, you'd be a millionaire by age 60. $300 is less than most car payments. If you're 35 and you contribute $400 a month, you'd still have over $850,000 at age 65, assuming a 10% return.

If you stick to something long enough and with enough persistence, momentum will take hold. Kay Yow, the great basketball coach, said, "What is delayed is not denied." Just because your goal hasn't been achieved in the time you expected it to be doesn't mean it won't happen in the future. Consistency over the long term can be the most difficult part of every endeavor.

Many people see a millionaire or a successful person and assume they've been that person their entire lives. But that's not what happened in most cases. That person started in a similar spot to you. The only difference is they figured out how to earn their money, keep their money, and grow their money.

Patience and consistency are key. Don't give up too soon, especially if you aren't seeing results immediately.

Being focused on something intensely for two days or two weeks, or even two months likely won't make a significant change in your life. Focus is staying on point or staying dedicated to that desire for the long term or until you achieve it.

Consistency is the key to any big goal. Consistent improvement counts. If we just make a small improvement each day, those tiny improvements add up to huge results by the end of a year or decade. I know that if you haven't experienced this firsthand, it's difficult to believe. I know this because I hadn't seen this in my life. I hadn't been consistent enough to see the rewards of consistency. But as I started my debt-elimination journey, I realized that the consistent extra payments toward my debt really made a dent in my balances. I saw that consistently spending less in different areas of my life allowed me to make bigger payments on my debt. I saw that when I performed consistently and continued with the same company instead of leaving when I got mad brought greater rewards.

It's the consistent, almost boring, behaviors that create the biggest bang. Believe me, this was not intuitive to me. I was the person in my twenties looking for the best return, trying out different directions for a month and then switching directions quickly. I never stuck with anything long enough to bear the fruit of the seeds I had planted. You need to plant a lot of seeds in one garden for that garden to grow great vegetables. If you plant a few seeds here and there, you're not going to grow one big garden; you're going to have random small plants in weird soils that don't get watered and eventually die. Instead, plant your seeds in one garden, water that garden and ensure the soil is nutrient filled. That's how you get the best results.

Take Your Retirement with You When You Leave

You are bound to leave a company at some point in your career. You most likely will leave multiple companies. When you do, don't let your retirement account sit in your former employer's investment brokerage.

Instead, research discount brokerages and choose one you like. There are many discount brokerages out there, including Fidelity, Vanguard, Schwab, and E-trade. These brokerages (and many others) offer free accounts, commission-free trades, and the ability to roll over retirement accounts. They offer both retirement accounts (IRA's) and non-retirement (brokerage) accounts where you can buy funds and hold onto them for the long term.

To roll over your balance to this new discount brokerage, either call their customer service line or get in touch with one of their financial advisors. Their goal is to make the process as simple for you as possible. Let them initiate the rollover and make sure you do not request your current investment brokerage to send you the check. Request the check be sent directly to your new discount brokerage. This will save you a lot of hassle moving forward. If you do receive the check at home, you only have a limited number of days to deposit that check into your new account. If you miss this deadline, you will be charged a 10% penalty (assuming you are less than 59 and a half years old) and taxes on that withdrawal. It's much easier to do the direct rollover, having your current investment company send the check to your new discount brokerage.

Remember, we want to keep things simple. You don't need five retirement accounts at five different investment companies from five old jobs. Instead, consolidate them all into one brokerage. The brokerage may bring them in separately, meaning you continue to have different accounts, but at least they are all in one place for you to see them.

Consolidate as much as you can. The accounts you roll over may have different tax treatments depending on whether you've used post or pre-tax contributions, which require separate accounts, but if tax treatments are the same, you should be able to consolidate them.

Simplify wherever you can. You don't need twelve credit cards, and you don't need five retirement accounts in five different investment brokerages.

You'll have more transparency on fees at the discount brokerages as well. When you leave your former employer, there is no benefit to keeping that money at the prior investment company. You don't need someone else to manage your money. Instead, do research on your own.

When you take on this responsibility instead of letting someone else do it, you'll be more motivated to learn about the investments within your portfolio. The responsibility lies with you. This is your money. Act like this is your money.

Retirement investing is your doorway to freedom and flexibility. The sooner you start, the more growth you will achieve over your lifetime.

Section 4: Progressive Debt
Balance Your Speed

Progressive debt is debt used to purchase appreciating assets. Recall, regressive debt takes you backwards. Regressive debt is debt used for depreciating assets or stuff with little resale value. Regressive debt literally creates a negative net worth.

Progressive debt, on the other hand, has the power to take you forward. I can't go as far as saying this type of debt is good, but I can say this is the best form of debt. This debt is borrowed against assets that theoretically will be worth more in the future, which offset the risk you're taking.

The best example is your first house. Very few people are going to save the entire purchase price in cash. Instead, they'll put down between 5% and 20%. Because real estate prices have historically grown, your equity in the property will increase not only with the debt you pay off, but also with the appreciation.

Progressive debt is the fourth stage. This stage shouldn't start until you're done paying off your regressive debt. This is tough for many people. Many of us, including me, jumped into real estate while we still had credit card, student loan, or vehicle debt. I was fortunate my fixer upper didn't sink me financially, but I was in no position to buy a house at that time.

Patience is hard, but it's smart. It's hard to wait for what you want. I totally understand, but in the long run, waiting and being smart about your investments will take you so much further than rushing into a purchase.

Before we dive into the logic behind progressive debt, let's first talk about how awesome cash is. When you no longer have regressive debt, you will be amazed at how quickly your checking account grows. All the money you were paying toward debt payments is now flowing into your checking account without future obligations. You could have been paying $1,000 to $4,000 per month in debt payments. Imagine your checking account growing that much each month. That's what happens when you don't have debt.

11: Cash is King

As you advance on this journey, your whole understanding of money will change. You won't have the same sense of urgency or temptation in buying things you once did. Your growing net worth will become more important than an extra purchase.

As your regressive debt dwindles, you'll start paying for things with cash, and you'll feel it. You'll have an emotional twinge when you need to spend an extra $50. It won't feel the same as it did when you were spending with debt.

You'll understand how much you worked for this cash and how much you're giving up in the future by spending it today. You'll only gain this clarity, however, when you start taking these actions, improving your discipline and your money.

You'll also realize you can pay for big things with cash. You can buy cars and real estate with the cash in your accounts. The craziest thing for me is, now that I can write a check for a new car, I don't want a new car. I respect that cash too much. I would have behaved very differently in my twenties.

When I was in debt, I didn't worry about swiping that card. I knew there was already a pile of debt, so what's one more charge? I couldn't feel the pain of paying off more debt in the future.

Remember how difficult it is to save for retirement because you can't see it? It's similar to paying for something with debt.

When you're avoiding your debt, you don't feel the impact today because you can't see it. However, when you pay for it with cash, it comes out of your account today, and it is tangible. You see it and you feel it.

Myth 11: You Need to Borrow to Make a Big Purchase

You can use cash for everything; it just takes patience.

It's natural to think you need a loan for a significant purchase, like real estate or a new vehicle.

I remember feeling the exact same way when I attended Dave Ramsey's Financial Peace University in my early twenties. He talked about saving up to buy a car outright. My salary was $22,500 at the time and I had student loans and other bills. I thought this was a ridiculous statement. *Who is going to save up and pay cash for a car?*

However, I was completely wrong. When you are debt free and patient, you can save up the cash. Instead of getting another loan, think of alternative ways to get what you want. How could you increase your income to save faster for that item?

Let's revisit my net worth tracker. As you can see, my cash balances weren't growing very quickly, but this was on purpose. I was focused on paying down my regressive debt.

I continued to live on very little and increased my income via my full-time job and side hustles. This illustration is one year after the previous illustration. I paid off $50,000 of regressive debt this year. At this point, I was putting every extra dollar toward my debt, including 100% of an annual bonus I received.

Look at my net worth. It increased by $70,000 in one year. It helped that the market grew quite a bit this year. Just think of the power you create when your focus is strong and consistent.

Assets	Value	Debts	Balance	Monthly	Interest Rate	Annual Interest
HSA	$50	Credit Card 1	$3,200	$30	0.00%	$ -
Checking	$300	Credit Card 2	$0	$0	0.00%	$ -
Savings	$0	Credit Card 3	$0	$0	0.00%	$ -
Total Cash	$350	Credit Card 4	$1,747	$100	0.00%	$ -
		Residence Mortgage	$55,456	$448	3.25%	$ 1,802
401k	$89,500	Vehicle Loan	$2,500	$30	0.00%	$ -
Jeep	$8,000	Student Loan 1	$27,353	$160	2.63%	$ 718
Property	$77,000	Student Loan 4	$6,500	$100	0.00%	$ -
Total Assets	$174,850	Total Debt	$96,756	$868		$ 2,520
Net worth	$78,094					

Paying for things in cash changes your mindset and your spending behavior. This was the largest my net worth had ever increased in a year. It was unbelievable to me at the time. I had a five-figure net worth and was closing in on six-figures.

When your first reaction to wanting something or to solving a problem is to find a solution you can pay for in cash instead of pulling out your credit card, you know you're making progress.

Cash

I know I just mentioned this, but it is worth repeating. Paying with cash allows you to feel the emotional loss of the cash. It's tangible. When you use cash, you have more willpower to resist impulse buys.

I recently talked to a colleague who worked in the cruise industry. He confirmed cruises are cashless on purpose. When people use credit cards, they spend more money. It doesn't feel as real as it does when it's cash. Cruises, like most companies, understand consumer behavior.

Once you understand what these companies already know, you have the ability to take back your power.

This is true for small purchases and large purchases alike, from a can of soda to real estate. It's also true whether you are buying for personal consumption or buying for your business.

When buying a potential flip property or any other business endeavor, you will make decisions differently if you are using your own cash. When paying with debt, you are more likely to take on higher risk. When you pay with cash, you slow down. You make sure you buy the right property for the right price. You add finishes that are appropriate for that area and don't over-spend. Using cash instead of debt helps you to make better decisions.

The other significant benefit to spending with cash is that you will never get into regressive debt again. You will never let debt take you backwards. You will never have a negative net worth. When you use cash, you understand the bondage that regressive debt creates.

Let's look at my tracker after another nine months. In these nine months, I paid off $33,000 of debt, and my net worth jumped up by $47,000. This is what happens when you get focused. You can see how making progress every year adds up. I wasn't debt free yet, but I was getting close. I only had $10,800 remaining of regressive debt.

Assets	Value	Debts	Balance	Monthly	Interest Rate	Annual Interest
HSA	$50	Credit Card 1	$0	$0	0.00%	$ -
Checking	$300	Credit Card 2	$0	$0	0.00%	$ -
Savings	$0	Credit Card 3	$0	$0	0.00%	$ -
Total Cash	**$350**	Credit Card 4	$1,000	$100	0.00%	$ -
		Residence Mortgage	$52,747	$448	3.25%	$ 1,714
401k	$103,474	Vehicle Loan	$0	$0	0.00%	$ -
Jeep	$8,000	Student Loan 1	$9,800	$160	2.63%	$ 257
Property	$77,000	Student Loan 4	$0	$0	0.00%	$ -
			$0	$0		
Total Assets	**$188,824**	**Total Debt**	**$63,547**	**$708**		**$ 1,972**
Net worth	**$125,277**					

This was the first time I'd ever had a six-figure net worth. I was two months away from being 36 years old. I was a late bloomer, but once I realized how to manage my spending, I caught on quickly.

When you start making traction, your motivation skyrockets. Your intensity increases because you are getting close to your goal. Think about the Olympic long-distance runners. They've run, in some cases, miles and miles, but in that last stretch, they give it everything they have and run faster at the end than any time during the race.

It was similar for me. This was a long journey and there were stretches where I was tired, but when I saw how much progress I'd made, it was completely worth it. I sped up for the finish line.

I Paid Off My Debt!

It took almost five years. This was the longest commitment I had made in my life. The consistency, hard work, and patience paid off. This was my tracker three months after the last tracker.

Assets	Value	Debts	Balance	Monthly	Interest Rate	Annual Interest
HSA	$50	Credit Card 1	$0	$0	0.00%	$ -
Checking	$44,700	Credit Card 2	$0	$0	0.00%	$ -
Savings	$0	Credit Card 3	$0	$0	0.00%	$ -
Total Cash	**$44,750**	Credit Card 4	$0	$0	0.00%	$ -
		Residence Mortgage	$0	$0	3.25%	$ -
401k	$119,469	Vehicle Loan	$0	$0	0.00%	$ -
Jeep	$8,000	Student Loan 1	$0	$0	2.63%	$ -
Property	$0	Student Loan 4	$0	$0	0.00%	$ -
Total Assets	**$172,219**	**Total Debt**	**$0**	**$0**		**$ -**
Net worth	**$172,219**					

I sold my house, the fixer upper, which I was able to use the proceeds to pay off the remaining regressive debt and my mortgage. I lived there for four years and decided I was ready to rent temporarily. Today I own real estate, but at this point in my life, my goals were different. I was simplifying as much as possible to work toward my next goal.

I mentioned this in a prior chapter, but it is worth saying again. Because I started investing in retirement at the beginning of this journey, I wasn't starting from scratch. I had $119,000 in my 401K. This gave me a head start to my next goal, becoming a millionaire. I was already one-tenth of the way there. This is why the Regressive Debt and Retirement Investing stages happen simultaneously. You've already got a positive net worth when you become debt free.

You'll also see a nice large balance in my checking account. To be completely honest, I was scared I might return to my old habits and blow through this money. I had just put in years of work to get rid of this debt, and I didn't want to lose it.

To protect it from myself, I put a large amount into a CD (certificate of deposit) at my bank. I knew I was missing out on potential returns in the stock market, but I was scared. I didn't want to repeat my penny stock mistake again. I didn't want to slip up and lose this money. Putting it into a CD was the best thing I could have done. This gave me time to learn about mutual funds, ETFs (exchange-traded funds), and index funds. I wasn't rushed. I didn't make rushed decisions.

After you've paid off your regressive debt, the first thing you should do is celebrate. Have a party, go on vacation, or just take some time off and relax. You've just accomplished a major feat. I'm serious. This is significant.

Realizing you don't owe a penny to anyone is the most freeing feeling. Weight will be lifted you didn't know existed. We normalize debt so much in our modern day that it seems crazy for someone to not have payments. But debt free should be the new normal.

Paycheck to Paycheck Cycle

By paying off my debt, I was progressively escaping the paycheck-to-paycheck cycle.

I remember working labor at a factory between college years, and the general manager of the site said he had the same money issues as the laborers. He most likely made six times the amount of the average laborer, but he was still living paycheck to paycheck.

And he isn't alone. There are many percentages quoted, but it seems that around 50% of people who make more than $100,000 a year live paycheck to paycheck.

If you're making less than this, you're probably thinking the same thing I was. *How can you make six-figures and still live paycheck to paycheck?*

We have been brainwashed by advertisements and our company cultures to want the luxuries of life. As you move up the ladder in a company, the norm is to upgrade to a bigger house, fancier cars, and more expensive clothes. It's easy to let your income slip through your fingers when you're not paying attention.

Avoid these common mistakes to avoid the paycheck-to-paycheck cycle.

- **Lifestyle Creep**

Most of us start with low-paying jobs. As I've mentioned, my first job out of college paid $22,500 a year. A year later I got a raise to $25,000. Another year later, I changed companies and started at $31,000.

Every time I earned a higher salary, my expenses went up. I upgraded my car to a truck. I bought nicer clothes. I spent more on the weekends.

It's natural to continue increasing our lifestyle as we earn more money. We don't want to live in that small apartment any longer. We don't want to drive that beater in front of our colleagues.

Instead of making quick decisions, slow down and be patient. Think about the consequences of continuing to increase your spending.

- **Stuck Habits**

The majority of lottery winners end up worse off than before they won the lottery. This seems irrational. How can more money put you in a worse position?

When you're accustomed to a certain income level, your bad habits are limited to what you can borrow.

When you gain income, lenders increase your borrowing limits, which results in more debt. This is why it's so dangerous to keep your bad money habits when you earn more money.

Bad habits become more extreme.

- **Deserving More Belief**

I had a colleague at an old job tell me she hired a cleaning service for her house. There is nothing wrong with this, but this person was in a lot of debt. She still had student loans, a car loan, and credit card debt.

She said she worked hard and didn't want to clean the house when she got home. She justified it to herself that she made a good income (which she did) and could pay someone else to clean her house.

She said she deserved it.

Of course, outsourcing work you don't like makes life easier, and in most cases, I'm a fan. However, when you have debt, extra expenses aren't the answer.

Thinking you deserve extra services when you can barely make your monthly payments is a sure way to never become wealthy.

- **Instant Gratification**

I know it's tempting to buy what you want when you want it.

We all have a part of us that wants new things. These feelings reinforce our desire to purchase something, because we know we will get instant pleasure from it. Continuing to give in to unbudgeted and unexpected instant gratification steals your income and leaves you trapped in the paycheck-to-paycheck cycle.

To escape the paycheck-to-paycheck cycle, pay off your regressive debt and save an emergency fund. These are the two keys to escaping this trap.

Action 11 – Save an Emergency Fund

Being dependent on your credit cards isn't the answer. I was the worst at this. I loved having them. They made me feel secure. I felt that if I needed anything or if anything unexpected came up, they were there. They were my security. Today I know the truth. Credit cards are not your security. If they are your lifeline, it's time to cut them up. By continuing to depend on them, you are continuing to accrue high interest charges and buy more than you need.

Real security is having cash in the bank. It's owning enough investments to never have to worry about money again. Cash is your security, not credit cards.

Having six to twelve months of expenses in cash gives you peace of mind. This cash acts as security, insurance, and freedom. If anything goes wrong in life, which it undoubtedly will, you've transformed an emergency into an inconvenience. If an appliance goes out, you've got the money to buy a new one. If you get into a minor accident, you've got the money to cover the cost.

I always have the urge to deplete my checking account and invest all my cash into stocks and index funds. I don't want my cash to sit there and do nothing. But that's the wrong way to look at it. When you have cash, it's there if the unexpected happens. It's a safety net. Sleeping is much better when you aren't constantly worried about money. Believe me, I didn't sleep well for years when I was trying to dig myself out of debt, but now I sleep very well.

Another benefit of keeping extra cash around is you can take advantage when the market tumbles. Anyone who had cash in 2008 or 2020 knows exactly what I mean. In 2008, if you had cash, you could buy real estate so cheaply and reap significant rewards just a few years later. In 2020, the stock market tumbled dramatically and quickly. If you had cash to invest, you could have seen amazing gains in less than a year. I was in a position where I had cash and reaped some of this volatile market's rewards.

Anti-fragile

Anti-fragile is a word I've seen a lot in recent years. Anti-fragile in this context is not being vulnerable to a job loss, a job change, or a sabbatical. It's having enough cash on hand to face any headwinds or costs in the future.

Letting this cash build up is the best thing you can do. It's good if you're a little scared like I was. A little fear can help you make better decisions. There is a fine line, however, between a little fear and fear running your life. If, after two years, all your money is still tied up in a CD because you're afraid of other appreciating assets, you may have crossed the line, allowing fear to run your life.

The good thing is you have cash though. Cash is much more fun than regressive debt. Having extra cash alleviates stress. When you have cash in the bank, you are not dependent on your job. You have options. You can take risks. Extra cash means you can battle a storm longer. Extra cash makes you anti-fragile.

When you are anti-fragile, you realize you have more control over your life than you previously did. The more cash and wealth you have, the more tangible your control is. Back in the Mindset stage chapters I mentioned how much control you have in your life. When you have a pile of debt and are living paycheck to paycheck, you feel trapped. You feel trapped at your job, trapped with your bills, and trapped by your debt. It's more difficult to believe you have control of your life. You can't see it. You can't feel it. Remember, when we can't see something or it isn't right in front of us, we have a hard time believing it.

When you become anti-fragile – regressive debt-free with cash in the bank – you feel more control over your life. You'll see it through your decisions.

12: Assets Make You Wealthy

My accounting professor defined an asset as something that brings future cash. Think about the assets of a company. There are fixed assets – machinery, equipment, vehicles – which give employees the ability to create products that generate profit and cash for the company. There is inventory, the actual products to be sold, which brings future cash to the company. And there are accounts receivable, which are invoices that have been sent to customers, but not yet paid.

Not all assets are created equal though. Some assets naturally appreciate over time and some naturally depreciate. Inventory is a depreciating asset. In most cases, as inventory gets older, it becomes less valuable. You see this in stores at the clearance rack. Those items have been in the store the longest and are being sold at a discount.

Machinery and equipment are depreciated every month based on the standard useful life. Even though this equipment is needed to produce products, it loses value every time it's used. It becomes less reliable as it ages.

You're not going to like this, but cash is a depreciating asset. If you sit on cash long enough, the value of that cash dwindles. Because of inflation, we can't buy what we once could with the same amount of cash.

Appreciating assets are the assets you want to accumulate. Real estate, land, stocks, and index funds are examples of popular appreciating assets. You are an appreciating asset yourself. How much cash do you bring in? Your mind, perspective, education, confidence, and skills determine how much cash you can earn. The more you invest in yourself, the more return you will experience.

On the other side of the equation are liabilities. My accounting professor defined liabilities as future cash outflows. In my company we have accounts payable, those invoices from vendors that haven't been paid. We have warranty provisions in case we need to pay for a claim, and we have payroll accruals for future cash payments to employees.

No one wants liabilities. Debt is a liability. Think about it. If you have a car loan, you're getting burdened twice: once by the depreciating value of the car, and once by the interest you're paying on the loan.

If your goal is to become financially free, it's time to start putting your money into appreciating assets and stop wasting your money on liabilities.

The key to becoming a millionaire is not only to earn money, but also to grow your money.

Myth 12: You Become Rich with Only Your Hard Work

<u>Your money needs to work for you.</u>

You can't become wealthy with the sweat of your own labor. There aren't enough hours in the day for you to work. We each only have 24 hours a day. We all get the same amount of time. Why is it that some people can earn so much more than others?

I used to think how cool it would be if I didn't need to sleep. I could work two full-time jobs and make double the salary. If I didn't need sleep, I'm not sure that working 16 to 20 hours a day is how I'd want to spend my time, but when I was young and broke, I thought it would've helped a lot. The thing is, we all need sleep. We all need time for relaxation. We all need time to be social.

Because of this, we need to figure out ways to make money that don't depend on our labor – what is generally referred to as passive income. It's the money you make in your sleep. Think about having rental income or making interest off your money at the bank. Other than a few calls, you don't need to work on these investments to generate income. This is the key to accumulating real wealth. In essence, your money is working for you when you invest it in appreciating assets.

The ultimate goal is to fund these appreciating assets with your cash. However, there will be times when you find an unbelievable deal on a property or business, and you don't have the cash. These are the opportunities where it may be wise to take on progressive debt.

For example, when I bought the fixer upper to live in, I was in no position to buy this place. However, by taking on progressive debt, I was able to buy it for $50,000 and sell it for $104,000 four years later. I spent $30,000 to renovate it and made $24,000 profit.

Assets Create Appreciation

Appreciating assets make you wealthy. Again, you only have so much time and energy to work. Instead of burning yourself out by working 80 hours a week, let your money work for you. One year after the last tracker my net worth grew to $330,000.

Assets	Value	Debts	Balance	Monthly	Interest Rate	Annual Interest
HSA	$400	Credit Card 1	$0	$0	0.00%	$ -
Checking	$25,348	Credit Card 2	$0	$0	0.00%	$ -
Business Checking	$40,000	Credit Card 3	$0	$0	0.00%	$ -
CD	$50,144	Credit Card 4	$0	$0	0.00%	$ -
Total Cash	**$115,892**	Residence Mortgage	$0	$0	3.25%	$ -
		Vehicle Loan	$0	$0	0.00%	$ -
401k	$182,141	Student Loan 1	$0	$0	2.63%	$ -
Truck	$32,000	Student Loan 4	$0	$0	0.00%	$ -
Property	$0					
Total Assets	**$330,033**	**Total Debt**	**$0**	**$0**		**$ -**
Net worth	**$330,033**					

It's absolutely amazing what compounding can do. Look at how much my 401K grew as well as my checking accounts. When you have no debt, all the money you were paying on payments is yours to keep.

I mentioned earlier I was afraid of losing that original $50,000 I had in my checking account. I didn't earn much interest in the CD, but I also didn't lose it. For me, I needed this transition period to learn about the different discount brokerages and what they offered. I ended up choosing one that suited me best. It offers mutual funds, index funds, and ETFs with no commissions on trades as well as single stocks. Their website provides historical performance of the funds and stocks as well as other research and ratings.

Full disclosure: I know you see growth on every one of these trackers, but I was updating this tracker almost every paycheck. I didn't see growth every two weeks. Some weeks my net worth fell. The market goes up and down. It can dip for months at a time. When it went through these dips, it was a little worrisome and demotivating, but I never stopped my investing habits. When I look back over the annual growth on these trackers, I am still amazed. The power of compounding works. I didn't really believe it until I saw it in my own accounts.

Action 12 – Analyze Opportunity Costs & Fees

Progressive debt means you are borrowing to buy an appreciating asset. When you borrow money, you pay extra fees and interest. Borrowed money makes your overall investment more expensive.

In many cases, your home is the reason for your progressive debt. For most people, their home represents the largest asset they will purchase as well as the largest debt they will incur. Owning a home is a huge accomplishment.

What comes with this opportunity, however, is opportunity costs. Opportunity costs occur when you decide to go in one direction. By making that decision you are giving up another direction.

For example, you have $10,000 in your bank account. If you choose to spend this $10,000 on a new car, then you are giving up the opportunity of investing this $10,000 in the stock market. Every decision you make creates an opportunity cost for another choice.

Choosing one direction means you simply can't choose another direction at that point in time. Opportunity costs aren't a bad thing. When you are committed to something, you don't care about other opportunities.

Once you've decided and understand the opportunity costs, it is then time to analyze the fees and interest that come with that decision.

In the regressive debt section, the formula below was illustrated which demonstrates whether refinancing is the right move.

Principal Balance	x	Current Interest Rate	x	Number of Years to Pay Off	>	Principal Balance	x	New Interest Rate	x	Number of Years to Pay Off	+	Loan Origination Fees	+	Prepayment Penalty

When you analyze whether it's beneficial to refinance, you are comparing the costs of the old loan to the costs of the new loan. You can use part of this formula when deciding to go for a new investment as well. The right side of the above formula stays the same. The right side of the formula gives you an indication of how much interest and fees you will pay for this debt.

Cost of Progressive Debt	=	Principal Balance	x	New Interest Rate	x	Number of Years to Pay Off	+	Loan Origination Fees	+	Prepayment Penalty

When buying your first home, this is something you should consider. You want to know how much this progressive debt is costing you each month. Remember, transparency in your money is the key to winning with your money.

You'll be surprised by how much interest you'll pay over a 30-year mortgage. This formula above is a simplified version, but I encourage you to find an online debt calculator to see the numbers. For example, on a $250,000 dollar home loan at 5% interest, you would pay $233,000 in interest alone. In other words, you would pay $483,000 for your home including the interest over 30 years. This doesn't include the closing costs, which can range upwards to $5,000. Fees and interest are expensive, especially when it comes to progressive debt.

If you choose to take on a 15-year mortgage instead, you will pay $106,000 in interest. This is a significant savings over the $233,000 above, however, this is still a high cost. In other words, you're paying $356,000 for your home.

When buying investment assets, there is another variable that's vital. The ROI (return on investment) tells you if the investment you're looking at is worth the risk. We'll look at ROI in detail in the next chapter.

Play the Long-Term Game

Many appreciating assets aren't liquid. Think about real estate. It takes 30 to 45 days to close in most states. Even with a cash buyer, it usually takes at least 10 business days. Time is an important piece of real estate transactions, but also the commissions and closing costs are significant. Many individuals use real estate agents. The standard real estate commissions consume 6% of your selling price. In addition, there are closing costs that can consume another 3%. That's 9% that could be consumed in the closing of the sale of your property.

Let's take a quick example. If you bought a property for $200,000 and six months later, it's worth $250,000, that sounds like an amazing appreciation in a short period of time. However, when you take 9% of the $250,000 sales price, that's $22,500 in closing cost and fees.

This means you aren't left with $50,000 profit; you are only left with $27,500 profit.

If you hold onto real estate for the long-term, you'll make much more money. It's the long-term appreciation that creates true wealth.

Real estate can be very lucrative. I personally love real estate. The market over the past few years has not been normal though. It was difficult to find a deal. Just about every property was selling at a premium. Before you purchase a property, do your research. Learn about the commissions and closing costs as well as the recurring expenses.

Stocks and stock-related investments are the most liquid of the appreciating assets we will dive into in this book. In many cases you could buy and sell them on the same day. There are a few problems with this short-term strategy though.

First, you can't time the stock market. Believe me, I have tried. I've gotten lucky a few times, but I'm not consistent. You won't be either. The best stock investors advise to invest in the long-term. The stock market has an excellent track record over the long term.

Second, if you buy and sell stocks within one year, you will pay ordinary income tax on your gains. Your ordinary income tax percentage is always higher than your capital gains percentage. If you hold onto your stock investments for at least a year, you will pay lower taxes on your gains.

Businesses are the third appreciating asset we will visit in the next section. Acquiring customers and optimizing strategies takes time. Investing in businesses is the least liquid of these three appreciating asset categories due to the nature of most businesses.

Keep a long-term mindset as you purchase appreciating assets. You will make better decisions and won't be rushed by impulses.

13: Risk Can be Healthy or Dumb

Debt creates risk. There is no exception with progressive debt. When you borrow money to make a purchase, you are taking on risk.

The first risk is you can't pay your payments. If you lose your job or your income is reduced, you may not have enough money to pay your bills. When you can't pay your bills, lenders start calling and could repossess or foreclose on your assets.

A lien is a right of ownership. When you take on debt to buy an asset like a house or vehicle, the lender puts a lien on your title or deed, meaning you don't own that asset outright. It means there are conditions that must be met in order for you to maintain ownership.

Think about it. If you didn't come up with 100% of the cash to purchase your asset, who did? That was the lender. They forked over quite a bit of money for you to gain possession of this asset. In return they are entitled to a lien on your property. Debt inherently creates risk – risk that you can't pay your bills and risk that you might lose your assets.

The second risk is your lender may recall your loan early, meaning they will require you to pay in full your entire balance at a certain point in time. This doesn't normally happen, but if lenders get into financial trouble, or their companies are purchased or merged with other lenders, then this scenario is possible.

If this happens, they will likely give you a grace period to refinance the loan elsewhere, but what if you've allowed your credit score to slip, or the value of your asset is less than the amount of your loan? It will be difficult to refinance with another lender. If you can't find another lender, then you'll need to pay the loan off in full. However, I assume you won't have the cash to pay off the lender, which is why you needed the loan in the first place.

Myth 13: Taking Risk is Dangerous

<u>You've got to take risks if you want to grow.</u>

Everyone has a different risk tolerance. I happen to be less risk-averse financially than my best friend, but she is much less risk-averse when it comes to other aspects of life.

Some of us can give a speech in front of an audience with no issue, and then there's me. I physically start shaking when I'm talking in front of people. It's funny how different we all are and how some things seem risky to some people and not to others.

The risk I'm referring to here is financial risk. Debt creates an obligation and produces more potential scenarios where our assets could be taken from us. However, I am debt free, but I am open to taking on progressive debt for the right risk. When you have a plan and are buying an appreciating asset, progressive debt can expedite wealth creation.

Investing in the stock market is also risky, but I highly recommend it. When you invest in mutual funds or ETFs with historically good returns, the risk you are taking is worth it. If you don't invest in the stock market or in other appreciating assets, what's the likelihood your money depreciates in value over the next 40 years? That's not a risk; that's a guarantee. Sometimes things that seem risky are the safer bet.

Risk creates return. Compounding doesn't work if you aren't earning a return. In the last chapter I mentioned the ROI (return on investment) calculation. Depending on the type of asset you have, your inputs will be slightly different, but the basic calculation is the same.

ROI	=	$\dfrac{\text{Current Value of Asset - Cost of Asset}}{\text{Cost of Asset}}$

In stock-related investments, we can literally calculate our ROI daily. We can see the prices the stocks are trading at. When choosing a fund, most brokerages provide historical information. You can see what that fund has earned over the last one year, five years, ten years, and life-to-date.

In a real estate flip, it's vital to know the renovation budget and the projected selling price estimates as these will tell you how much you can pay for the property, while maintaining a decent ROI.

For example, if you see a property listed for sale at $100,000, but it needs $60,000 of work and would likely sell for $175,000 after the renovation, this isn't a great deal. When you factor in the closing costs of $16,000, you have a negative return on investment, as illustrated below.

$176,000 = $100,000 + $60,000 + $16,000

ROI	=	$\dfrac{\$175,000 - \$176,000}{\$176,000}$	=	-0.6%

Now, what if you could buy this same property for $75,000 instead of $100,000. That changes the return significantly. You're making a great return at almost 16%.

$151,000 = $75,000 + $60,000 + $16,000

ROI	=	$$\frac{\$175,000 - \$151,000}{\$151,000}$$	=	15.9%

One caveat is that I'm assuming this 16% happens within a year. If this flip takes three years, then your annualized return on investment would be much lower. It would be closer to 5% a year, which is okay, but not great. Just like time is an important component of compounding, it is also a significant variable in calculating your returns.

Recall if you put your money under your mattress for 20, 30, or 40 years, that cash is being eaten by inflation. That $20,000 you spent on a new car 10 years ago will no longer buy that car today. Inflation eats up the value of your money, and over the long term will reduce the value significantly.

In addition, you won't have the opportunity to experience compounding. The stock market and other appreciating assets might feel risky, but what are you losing if you don't take this risk? The opportunity costs of not investing creates a very difficult environment to become financially free.

There are risks to taking on debt. There are risks to investing. You take risks every day when you interact with the world. Life is all about taking risks within certain boundaries. When you understand the risk, you can mitigate many potential losses.

Let's look at some actions you can take to mitigate the risk of progressive debt.

Your First Home

If you've followed the 5 stages of money, then you are regressive debt free when you purchase your first home.

Don't let your emotions dictate your decision and the price you're willing to pay. Too many people get caught up with the dream of owning their own home and lose all rationality. They let their emotions dictate the price they are willing to pay. They have a picture in their head of how amazing this specific home is, and no other house can give them the same value. They focus on this one home and go all-in, creating a bidding war. In the end, if the property doesn't appraise for the value they agreed to buy it for, they are left bringing more money to the closing table than originally expected. In the excitement of the bidding war, they also maxed out the amount the lender had approved them for. They don't care though. They won. They got the house they were after.

Visit this couple a year later and ask them how they feel about the home. They might still love it, but they are putting a huge percentage of their paycheck into this house every month. They don't have extra funds for vacations or retirement investing, because all their money is being sucked into this house. This couple finally sees that this house isn't that special. They could have been just as happy on the other side of town, where prices are lower.

You don't want to be in the position where 50% of your monthly income is going toward your mortgage, taxes, and home insurance. This is not a fun way to live.

A better rule of thumb is to keep your housing at less than 30% of your gross monthly income.

Leverage

The term, leverage, is used when someone takes on debt to buy an appreciating asset. Using progressive debt is leveraging your investment.

One of my friends took full advantage of leverage back in 2009 when the housing prices crashed. Housing prices were so low at this time. It's almost unbelievable now. She found a lender that only required her to put down 3% on each of the houses she purchased. She leveraged these properties big time. She did a ton of research. She found the right areas and the right property managers. She made a great income on the rents while she owned the properties, and she profited significantly when she sold the properties at double and triple the prices. This is the right way to use leverage. She had other cash reserves as back up if any of these loans went south. This is how to use leverage to your advantage.

When assets are priced low and no one else is buying, that's when you make your move. She took on a lot of risk by leveraging 97% of the loans, but it worked out for her. The more the properties appreciated, the more profit she made.

Leverage creates more risk for both you and the lender. Leverage has the power to create wealth faster but can also create losses faster.

Leverage can also be used to buy stocks and foreign currency. Most brokerages require you to get additional approval to use their leverage. You can basically buy double the stock with the same amount of cash, but this is very risky. I was tempted to try this a few years ago, but decided it was too risky for me. As we saw the market fizzle in 2022, I'm happy I didn't do this. I would have been sold out of my positions. Instead, I kept my shares and weathered the storm by holding onto them.

Don't leverage stock investments. Progressive debt on stock investments is not smart. The stock market is much more volatile than the real estate market. They both represent appreciating assets, but they are very different. Stocks, mutual funds, and ETFs are vulnerable to people's perceptions of the economy and to all the variables impacting companies. They can change 20%-50% in a day based on a news headline. These assets are much more liquid than real estate, and individuals have the ability to click the 'buy' or 'sell' button from their personal computers. The risk of progressive debt on stock-related assets is too high.

When borrowed money is fueling your investment account, you are more emotional as well. This means you will sell a gain quicker than you would a loss. What this results in is a lot of very small gains and very large losses. You hold onto your losses longer, but you sell your winning stocks faster.

When emotions and debt are combined, you are not going to win in the stock market. Instead, do not leverage your stock investments. Only use leverage with real estate.

Never Co-Sign a Loan

Progressive debt is one level of risk, but co-signing a loan for someone else is a completely different level. Never, never co-sign a loan for someone else. When you co-sign a loan, it means you are taking responsibility for paying that debt even if the asset isn't in your name. The asset could be a vehicle or real estate.

Of course, the person asking you to co-sign tells you that you will never have to worry about it, but what happens when they lose their job or decide to move away with the car? It's a nightmare for all involved.

I saw this a lot at the bank. You think you're helping this person build their credit or get back on their feet, but you aren't helping. Remember, regressive debt takes you backwards. You are helping them create negative net worth. You're not helping them. There is a reason they can't get the loan on their own.

When I graduated from college, I wanted a new car. I drove an old Honda Accord and thought I was ready for a newer car. I went to the dealership and found one I liked. The problem was I didn't have a job. I went with the understanding that my mom was going to co-sign the loan for me. I filled out some paperwork, and when I got home, my mom wouldn't do it. She said she never agreed to that. I was annoyed. I had to call the dealership and tell them she wouldn't co-sign for me. Even though I was mad about it, it was the best thing for me. It took longer than expected to find a decent job after I graduated. I don't know how I would have made those payments.

Debt and Taxes

I'm sure you've heard someone bragging about how much they are saving on their taxes because they are keeping their mortgage. You might even get this advice from your financial advisor. Do you ever think about the incentives driving the financial advisor?

If you pay off your mortgage, you'll have less to invest with his company. Financial advisors generally make commission based on a percentage of the total money they are managing. If you take that $200,000 you've been investing and pay off your house, your advisor's commissions are going to decrease.

Instead of taking this advice as truth, remember everyone has different incentives. In many cases, you can do the math and see if what they are saying is accurate.

When you do the math, you'll see the strategy to keep debt on real estate and other assets to save taxes is an illogical strategy. Think about it. You're paying interest on your house at a certain percentage. Let's say it's 4% of a $200,000 mortgage balance. That is $8,000 every year you are paying in interest. When you add the interest to your Schedule A on your tax return, that deduction reduces your overall taxable income.

Let's say your taxable income before this interest deduction is $90,000. If you're filing status is married filing jointly, your tax is $11,300 (per the 2022 tax tables). After this deduction, your taxable income is only $82,000, which means your tax is $9,500. This means you saved $1,800 in taxes.

Great, you saved $1,800 in taxes, but you paid $8,000 in interest. I see that as a $6,200 loss overall. You paid your lender an extra $8,000 and paid the government $1,800 less.

When you make decisions, make sure the math works.

Action 13 – Prove You're Committed with a Down Payment

There is a reason you're taking on progressive debt. Usually, it's to buy your first house, but it could also be to purchase an investment property or a business. Whatever it is, make sure you are committed to this investment. The way you do this is to provide a down payment with your own cash. Most lenders will require a down payment anyway, but it's still worth stating here.

When you have something to lose from your investment, you'll know if this is something you're willing to commit to. This also shows the lender you are personally invested in this asset, which removes some of their risk. They will generally reward you with a lower interest rate if your down payment is large enough.

Section 5: Non-Retirement Investing
Reach for the Sky

You've done it. You've made it to the final stage of money, the Non-Retirement Investing stage.

To recap, once you've paid off your regressive debt, it's time to bump up your retirement contributions. Between 10% and 20% is a great range. You may also have a house at this point. Work toward paying this house off early.

When you no longer have debt payments, your paycheck comes with more options, and cash accumulates faster in your checking account. The question is, what do you do with this cash?

You can save up for future purchases and you can invest.

We'll dive into the most popular appreciating assets in this section. The direction you go is based on your desired time, energy, and interest.

For example, if you're looking for less time-consuming assets, then I suggest the stock market. Index funds, low-cost mutual funds, ETFs, and dividend-paying stocks are all great options. These are about the most passive you can get when it comes to income.

If you're looking for something more hands-on, real estate might be the direction for you. Renting and flipping are the most common strategies within real estate investing. Both require more time and potentially hands-on work depending on your approach.

The final avenue we'll discuss is investing in businesses. I'm not talking about the indirect investment via stocks. I'm talking about a bigger piece of ownership in the business, potentially owning the entire business. This can be as hands-on as you make it. This type of investment requires more time at the beginning until systems are created and managers are hired.

There are so many options when you start accumulating money. The key is to not rush. If you don't know what you want to invest in, do what I did. Put it into a saving account until you really know. It's much better to miss out on a year of potential returns than to quickly invest it in something you'll regret later.

14: The Next Lap

Letting your cash build up in your checking account for years is not the answer to financial freedom. It depreciates over the long run. This is the most difficult way to become a millionaire. Your cash isn't working for you; it's working against you.

I'm currently finishing up a renovation of a new house. Many projects have required rework. For example, we finished tiling the shower and then tested the water. One of the hoses wasn't clamped tight, and we had a leak. We made a lot of progress forward, but then had to cut a hole in the drywall to fix the leak which meant we had to fix the drywall and repaint it. In other words, we went two steps forward and one step back.

When you depend on your own labor for wealth creation, you are going two steps forward and one step backward as inflation eats up the value of your money.

Over the next chapters we will look at specific assets where your money can grow without much effort from you, but first let's take a closer look at millionaires.

You have a picture in your mind of the typical millionaire. You used to think of fancy cars, extravagant houses, and lavish yachts, but if you've been reading, you now have a different image. The typical millionaire doesn't spend much money in proportion to their net worth. They invest their money instead. They don't live in the biggest houses or drive the most expensive cars. They aren't recognizable on the street. They drive their cars longer. This is the average millionaire today.

Myth 14: Most Millionaires are Celebrities

<u>**The vast majority of millionaires are not celebrities.**</u>

Many celebrities are millionaires, but most millionaires are not celebrities. Do you ever think about a professional athlete's window of opportunity to make money with their athletic ability? Many athletes are done playing sports by their mid-30's. Between college and retirement, they have about 15 years to make enough money to last them a lifetime. We see the largest contracts flashing in the news feeds and assume all professional athletes are making big bucks, but those are the exceptions.

The majority of professional athletes make what we would consider a healthy income, but remember they spend their time around other athletes making much more. Think about yourself. If your coworkers earned triple and quadruple your salary, would you try to live in similar houses as them and drive similar cars? It's the same peer pressure for athletes making much less than their teammates. They are in the spotlight, and it's easy for them to overspend. When they try to keep up the same lifestyle as their flashy peers, they end up spending most of their income, being left with very little.

Recall, if someone is making $400,000 and spending $370,000, they are worse off than someone earning $100,000 and only spending $40,000. The professional athlete has only $30,000 to invest whereas the average person has $60,000 to invest. Who's going to become a millionaire faster?

You don't need to be a celebrity. You don't need to inherit money. I know it seems out of reach right now, but as you make progress on your debt, and eventually your investments, you will see how possible this is.

There have been various research studies done throughout the years confirming these truths. Most millionaires didn't inherit their money; they saved and invested over the long term. They didn't fall for get-rich-quick schemes. They didn't cripple themselves with debt. The facts speak for themselves.

Anyone can become a millionaire.

And that includes you.

You've seen the mistakes I've made with money. I took out student loans. I cashed out retirement early. I maxed out credit cards. I fell for instant gratification. I bought things I couldn't afford.

The awesome thing about life is even though we make mistakes, we all can change our behavior. We can change our beliefs. We can change our perspective. We have so much power within us. We decide what choices we make every day.

Millionaire Habits

A high percentage of millionaires became millionaires through their retirement accounts, primarily their 401k or 403b. The simplest, logical conclusion is that you can become a millionaire through your retirement accounts as well.

When I started getting serious about my money, I researched and read anything I could about the topic. I remember reading about the habits of millionaires, and a few habits stuck out to me.

- **Millionaires wake up early.**

Many millionaires wake up about three hours before they start their workday. Some people have more energy in the morning, and some are night owls. Find your most productive hours and mold your sleeping schedule around those hours.

An extra hour in the morning is productive for me. I have time to write and plan my day, whereas an extra hour in the evening would likely be spent in front of the television.

- **Millionaires don't watch much TV.**

If you're spending hours every day glued to the television, there is a good chance you're wasting time. We only get so much time in this life and none of us know how much we get.

Millionaires realize that watching TV is not a productive use of time. You're basically zoning out and living through someone else's life. I do like to watch TV, but it's generally not multiple hours every day.

- **Millionaires read a lot.**

Reading can be healing, educational, inspiring, and entertaining. Reading makes your mind work. As you read words, you create pictures in your mind. Reading gives you new insights and sparks ideas.

It doesn't matter if it's fiction or non-fiction. Find a topic you're interested in and read another book this week. Your mind will thank you.

- **Millionaires don't look like millionaires.**

I learned this through Thomas Stanley's *The Millionaire Next Door*. This one seemed the most interesting to me. Millionaires don't spend all their money on consumption. They watch what they spend and keep their lifestyle at bay. Millionaires understand the value of a dollar and don't let their dollars slip through their hands.

My friend and I were flipping a house a few years ago, and we needed lunch. We had been in demolition mode and were dirty. We went to a sub shop to eat. A family came in and gave us weird looks. I enjoyed it, because I knew we had much more net worth than they did, but I also knew we looked dirty. Never judge a book by its cover.

- **Millionaires use the power of compounding.**

Compounding is said to be the eighth wonder of the world for a reason. It's astounding how fast your money grows over the long term.

Let's revisit that original example. You put $500 a month in an index fund or a cheap mutual fund, or you put $500 under your mattress. That's $6,000 per year. In 40 years, you could have $240,000 under your mattress or you could have over $1,600,000 at an 8% return if you had invested it.

$500 a month is a car payment today. You can afford to invest $500 a month if you're paying for that car. People don't take advantage of this because they don't believe the numbers. The math works though. I'm a millionaire today – primarily because of compounding in my 401k.

Millionaires are patient.

This one is the most difficult for me. Anyone that knows me knows that I am not a patient person. I like to get things done. I like to get them done as efficiently as possible. I don't like to waste time.

I especially didn't like to waste time driving. When I moved back to Ohio from Los Angeles, I was driving a lot. I had moved to a new town and needed to drive a decent distance to see friends and family. Being accustomed to driving in LA and never getting a ticket, I had forgotten how strict the cops were in Ohio. Within a year I had accumulated six speeding tickets. I received a letter from the state of Ohio saying they would suspend my license if I got one more ticket.

Luckily, I drive slower these days and do a lot less driving. My patience is growing as I get older. I finally see how patience pays off. I see how my money grows when I don't touch it. I see how my career grows when I stay at the same company. Patience is the key.

The story of the tortoise and the hare is accurate. The tortoise always wins the race, because he's patient and stays focused on this one race the entire time. Meanwhile, the hare is fast but is prone to distraction. Strive to be the tortoise on your way to becoming a millionaire.

7 Streams of Income

The IRS did a study of over 6,000 individuals and confirmed the average millionaire has 7 streams of income.

These include the following:

1. Earned income (salary from a job)
2. Rental income (rents from real estate)
3. Dividend income (dividends from stocks)
4. Capital gains (selling appreciating assets)
5. Profits (owning businesses)
6. Interest income (interest on savings, CD's)
7. Royalty income (selling rights to something they created)

When you have multiple streams of income, you are no longer dependent on one income, and you earn more money. The key to becoming a millionaire is to start thinking like a millionaire.

Increasing my income expedited my journey in big ways. Although more income is the key, there are very different approaches based on where you are financially.

If you still have regressive debt, then a part-time job is the best option for you. A part-time job is a guaranteed paycheck.

For example, when I purchased the fixer upper at the beginning of this journey, the property needed a lot of work. I worked at Lowes part-time on the weekends. During this phase I spent 20 hours every weekend at Lowes, at least 40 hours every week at my full-time job, and many hours working on the property. Even though it was a lot of work, it was temporary, and I collected an extra paycheck and saved with employee pricing on products I was going to buy anyway with the remodel.

There are an unlimited number of part-time gigs available, from retail to delivery to bookkeeping, tutoring and so forth. You can likely make much more than I did at Lowes, but you've got to be willing to work.

After you've paid off your regressive debt, you have the option to start a small business side hustle. The biggest difference with a small business is you aren't guaranteed a paycheck. Small businesses also require some type of investment upfront. Examples are starting a lawn care company where you need to purchase a lawnmower or starting an online store where you'll need to pay for inventory. The number of small business ideas is endless.

The biggest difference between a part-time job and a small business side hustle is you can earn unlimited money with a side hustle. Although you aren't guaranteed a paycheck, the only thing stopping you from earning more in a side hustle is finding more customers.

In many cases, side hustles create income in categories 2, 5, and 7. I've personally made money from all 3 of these categories.

My business profits came from flipping real estate. After I paid off my debt, I started flipping properties. The first one was a real risk. The property was in a horrible state. I convinced a friend to do this project with me, which helped financially. I only had to come up with 50% of the purchase price and 50% of the renovation costs.

We ended up making $35,000 on this flip. This wasn't easy money though. Making this money meant almost every weekend at this property for 9 months.

We did another flip a year later and made about $25,000 on it, but it took 10 months.

I've also earned income from rental real estate. I've owned two rental properties throughout the years. I know people who do very well with rentals. In many cases these individuals have retired early. The key is to do your research. Find a deal. Don't overpay. And do thorough background checks on your potential tenants.

Regarding royalty income, I've written a few books and earn a small royalty every time a book is sold. I've created courses online where I continue to receive a percentage of each course sold. When it comes to royalty income, again, the opportunities are endless.

You could design T-shirts and sell them. You could create videos for YouTube. You could write a book or design a low content book like a journal and sell it on Amazon via KDP (Kindle Direct Publishing).

You can create various products and sell them on Gumroad. You can create courses on any topic you'd like and sell them on Udemy. You can offer services on Fiverr or Upwork. Don't feel limited with how you can make extra money.

This was my net worth a year after the last tracker. My net worth increased by $86,000 during this year. My 401k was steadily growing, but the biggest change was selling the flip property. I was able to put some of the profits back into the business checking account and invest some of those profits into my discount brokerage account.

Assets		Debts	Balance	Monthly	Interest Rate	Annual Interest
HSA	$1,500	Credit Card 1	$0	$0	0.00%	$ -
Checking	$45,300	Credit Card 2	$0	$0	0.00%	$ -
Business Checking	$52,000	Credit Card 3	$0	$0	0.00%	$ -
Discount Brokerage	$72,668	Credit Card 4	$0	$0	0.00%	$ -
Total Cash	**$171,468**	Residence Mortgage	$0	$0	3.25%	$ -
		Vehicle Loan	$0	$0	0.00%	$ -
401k	$210,090	Student Loan 1	$0	$0	2.63%	$ -
Truck	$35,000	Student Loan 4	$0	$0	0.00%	$ -
Property	$0					
Total Assets	**$416,558**	**Total Debt**	**$0**	**$0**		**$ -**
Net worth	**$416,558**					

Just a heads-up, not every side hustle I tried worked. I didn't stick with many of them long enough. There were some I wasn't committed to, and others just plain failed.

If your first try doesn't work, don't stop. There is something out there for you. It takes a while to understand your own skill set and what you have to offer to the world.

The key is not to give up. Keep performing well at your full-time job, while also figuring out what side hustle is right for you. It's going to be hard work in the short term, but I promise you, it will be worth it in the long term.

Action 14 – Invest in Non-Retirement Assets

It's time to put your money to work. Let your money generate its own income via appreciating assets. You have options when considering where to put this growing balance. The three most common appreciating assets are real estate, stock-related investments, and your own business.

Here are a few guidelines when starting:

- **Invest in something you understand.**

Whichever direction you decide, make sure you do your research. Understand exactly what you're putting your money into. Ask questions. Play the skeptic. Read books. Find online resources. Talk to experts.

A good test to see if you really understand what you're investing in is explaining it to a 5-year-old. Can you succinctly simplify your investment so that a 5-year-old could understand it? That's how well I want you to know it.

- **Invest with a long-term mindset.**

Unless you're flipping real estate, it's preferable to hold onto assets for at least a year. This reduces your tax rate. Selling these assets within a year result in being taxed at your ordinary income rate. If you hold onto these assets for over a year, then you will be taxed at the capital gains rate which ranges from 0% to 20% but averages 15% for most people.

The longer you leave your money in index funds, the more it will grow and compound. As we saw earlier, your money doesn't just grow linearly, it multiplies as it compounds upon itself year after year.

- **Invest without your emotions.**

The stock market is volatile. It goes up and down daily, hourly, and even by the minute. When you let your emotions lead your investment strategy, you're going to watch the market all day long. As the market tics down, you're going to panic. This isn't the way to invest. Find an index fund, deposit your money, and leave it alone.

We live in an unperfect world. Some days are bad. Some months are bad. However, look over the last few decades. Have there been any 10-year periods where the market didn't recover? Look at the 5-year periods. There are very few where the market didn't recover.

The market in total has always come back. Yes, it fluctuates, but it also grows. And it can grow a lot when things are good.

You've worked so hard to get to this point. You're ready. Don't shy away from this amazing opportunity. Find appreciating assets that appeal to you and get started.

15: Accumulate Appreciating Assets

The goal now is to focus on appreciating assets. The more appreciating assets you own, the more opportunities your wealth has to grow.

This is your time to figure out what investments appeal to you the most. You may love rental real estate and the monthly income provided by your tenants. You may love the hands-off aspect of investing in index funds. Or you may want to own a business. There is an endless amount of appreciating assets within real estate, stocks, and businesses.

Think about owning a business. You could own a construction company, a digital marketing firm, a restaurant, a truck driving company, an accounting firm, a franchise, etc. Don't feel limited by your options. The options for appreciating assets are endless.

Myth 15: Millionaires Make $1M Income Every Year

Millionaires are not defined by their income.

Millionaires are defined by their net worth. When someone's assets are $1,000,000 greater than her liabilities, she is considered a millionaire.

Many millionaires already know appreciating assets are the vehicle to grow their money, therefore most millionaires own real estate, some type of investment account, and maybe even a business or two.

People that gain their wealth too fast, like lottery winners or professional athletes put their money into depreciating assets, such as cars, clothes, vacations, TV's, computers, and speakers. Why do you think they end up with nothing? They put their money in assets that lose value. What happens when the cars are 10 years old, and the TV is outdated? They sell or scrap those originals at a loss and buy more, which eats away at their money.

There is a great story about Shaq. When he earned his first million dollars, he spent it immediately. He didn't completely blow it though. He paid off his parents' car loans and house loan, which was an awesome act of generosity. He knew most athletes didn't have money at the end of their professional careers. He decided he would be different. He invested in a ton of assets. He owns many Five Guys restaurants, car washes, Auntie Anne's, and gyms. He literally built an empire.

Ratio of Assets

Many people want to know what the best mix of appreciating assets is. The answer is there is no one size fits all. Remember, we are all different and value different things. You might be someone who doesn't want to think about your investments daily while someone else wants a completely hands-on approach.

I personally have about 50% in retirement investment accounts, 40% in real estate, and 20% in non-retirement investment accounts today. My plan is to continue increasing my discount brokerage accounts as I will need some income between the age I officially retire and when I turn 59 and a half, which is when I can withdraw from the retirement accounts.

Depending on which assets appeal to you, you most likely want to diversify. In other words, don't put all your money in one spot. For example, your money could be invested in the stock market, but don't only buy one stock. There are different levels of advice for this, but you probably don't want more than 5% to 10% of your assets to be in one stock. If you own index funds, you have built-in diversification, especially if you invest in funds that mimic the S&P 500. There are funds, however, that are made up of specific sectors. For example, I own one that is only made up of technology stocks. Even though there is some diversification built in, the technology sector tends to ebb and flow together.

Make sure you understand what stocks are included in your mutual funds or ETFs when you purchase them. Index funds provide the best diversification in the simplest form. This is why these are attractive to so many people.

You may love real estate investing and have all your money in rental properties. If this is your interest and you like the consistency of the monthly rental income, then go in this direction. Rental properties require more time than investing in index funds, but if you're a person who wants tangible assets, this may be the right path for you.

Maybe you have a business already, and this business is your life. You reinvest into this business instead of investing elsewhere. That's a great path as well. Like I said, this is not a one-size-fits-all. You are an individual with unique preferences. Find the type of appreciating assets that appeal to you the most and focus on them. Be less concerned with your ratios and more attentive to your assets.

Investing in the Stock Market

There are many strategies when it comes to investing in the stock market, from index funds to dividend-paying stocks and growth stocks.

Index Funds

The first and most passive approach to accumulating appreciating assets is investing in index funds. If this is your preferred approach, find a large discount brokerage, such as Fidelity, Schwab, Vanguard, or E-trade. There are many other discount brokers as well. Do some research to see which company appeals to you. In most cases you can open an account online and transfer the money from your checking account easily. Within this account, you can buy various funds and stocks, including index funds, low-cost mutual funds, ETFs, and single stocks.

Index funds come in the form of mutual funds and ETFs. They are a combination of many stocks brought together to mimic specific indexes, such as the S&P 500 or the Russell 2000, meaning they should grow roughly in line with that index. Index funds are very popular in that Warren Buffett and John Bogle, two well-known investors, gave the advice to invest in these.

Index funds are also popular with the FIRE (Financially Independent Retire Early) movement. Holding an index fund in your portfolio creates diversification instantly. When you buy a fund that mimics an entire index like the S&P 500, you are buying the 500 largest companies in the United States from a market capitalization perspective. You will still experience volatility, but this volatility is market and economy-driven instead of company-driven. Of course, some companies within the S&P 500 will go down in price and some will go up, but over the whole, their losses and gains counterbalance with each other, reducing your overall risk.

Mutual funds include index funds, but not all mutual funds are index funds. Mutual funds can also target specific industries or companies. For example, there are mutual funds that only consist of technology companies or energy companies. There are mutual funds that only include growth companies. Mutual funds are professionally managed. Make sure you look for low-cost mutual funds with historically good rates of return (usually above 10% for the last 10 years). If you've opened your account with a large discount broker, you can go to their website and search for mutual funds to look at their historic return over the last 5, 10, and 20 years. Most brokerages show each mutual fund's ratings as well as the historical returns and the expense ratios. Look for expense ratios of 0.25% or less. The lower the expense ratio, the less fees associated with the fund. Spend time comparing the different funds.

Another thing to know about mutual funds is when you sell them, you won't know the price you're selling at until the close of that trading day. It took me a while to understand this, but it's generally not a big deal, especially if you don't plan to sell very often.

ETFs (exchange traded funds) are like mutual funds in that they are baskets of stocks from multiple companies in the same industry or within similar phases of their life cycles. The primary difference with ETFs is they aren't managed like mutual funds. They can be bought and sold at any time while the market is open. In other words, if you want to sell your shares at 1pm, then you can sell them at 1pm. You'll get immediate confirmation instead of having to wait until the end of the trading day. ETFs also generally have lower expense ratios because they are not professionally managed. However, don't skip the step of checking their expense ratios, because there are some expensive ETF's as well.

Any of the above choices are great options for consistently investing over time. Now that you have more cash at your disposal, maybe you decide 5% of your income will go toward these accounts. If you are planning to retire early and are not sure where to start, contributing to an index fund is your best option. Based on history, the major indexes have grown over time. Yes, there have been some dips along the way, but look at the long-term trend when you do your research. Their overwhelming trajectory is up.

Dividend-Paying Stocks

Another strategy is dividend-paying single stocks. Just to warn you, this is riskier than buying index funds. One major upheaval within a company could tank your entire balance.

The best way to mitigate this risk is to not let one company's stock make up more than 5% of your investment portfolio.

The approach I use to find the right dividend-paying companies for me is to start with the Dividend Aristocrats and Dividend Kings list.

Dividend Aristocrats are companies with 25 years of consecutive dividend growth and included in the S&P 500. Some examples are Johnson & Johnson, IBM, Sherwin Williams, 3M, Walmart, Exxon Mobil, Procter & Gamble, and Coca-Cola. These companies have weathered storms throughout the years and are still able to grow their dividend consistently every year.

Dividend Kings are companies which have paid out growing dividends over the last 50 years. Some dividend kings are smaller companies, meaning they aren't dividend aristocrats, because they don't make the S&P 500 cut. Some dividend king examples are Grainger, Stanley Black & Decker, Sysco, Black Hills, Lowes, and Target.

You may see the dividend yield on these companies and wonder why dividends are such a great investment. For example, today the dividend yield of JP Morgan Chase is 2.68%. You can earn a higher interest rate in many high-yield accounts right now. Why would anyone choose dividends over a high-yield savings account?

The key is what happens in the long term. Let's say you buy one share of JP Morgan Chase at $150. Assuming they maintain their dividend per share for the next year, you will receive $4.02 over the next four quarters. Let's say in year two, the stock price is at $185, and they hold the 2.68% dividend yield, meaning they've increased the dollar value of the dividend per share. In this case, you own the same share, but you will earn $4.95 that year in dividends.

Because you bought the share in the prior year when the stock price was lower, your cost basis is still $150, but you earned $4.95, which equates to a 3.3% return, not the 2.68% stated dividend yield. This is the real power of dividends. When you buy growing companies over the long run and hold onto them for the long term, your personal return grows significantly.

To be eligible for the dividend, you must hold the stock on certain dates. Companies announce their next dividend on the declaration date. In this announcement, they confirm the ex-dividend date which is the date you must own the shares by to be eligible for the dividend payment. The payable date (or the date of the dividend payment) will also be announced on the declaration date. These dates almost always fall around the quarterly earnings release.

Some companies pay dividends monthly and annually, but most companies pay dividends quarterly.

Growth Stocks

Growth stocks are those companies who are anticipated to grow significantly. We've seen recent spikes in Tesla and Meta, which are two popular growth stocks. In many cases these are less established companies with higher-than-average volatility. These stocks can produce significant returns, however, they come with higher risk. They can also fall fast.

This is where understanding a company's financials and competitive advantage is critical. In the past, the P/E ratio was used to determine if a company was undervalued or overvalued. This price to earnings ratio compares the current stock price to the earnings per share of the company. Looking at today's P/E ratios, you'll realize this isn't the best indicator of the stock value any longer. There are other factors that play into the value.

Understanding the current products, the market share, and the strategy for where the company is going is also critical to finding the most undervalued growth stocks.

These are only three strategies for stocks, but there are many more out there. Do some research. If the stock market is interesting to you, find the strategy that energizes you the most.

No matter which strategy you go for, be in it for the long-term. As Warren Buffett famously said, "you haven't lost anything until you sell." Be patient. Ride out the waves. Give your money time to grow.

Diving into Real Estate

Real estate is another great option when it comes to non-retirement investing. If you're not a fan of the stock market, and you'd like to have more tangible assets, real estate might be for you.

Real estate is hands-on relative to stock investing. If you go the renting route, even if you hire a property manager, there are decisions you'll need to make. Lots of situations arise, such as a tenant isn't paying their rent on time, or they cause damage, or they get hurt on the property. These scenarios need proper attention. If you go the flipping route, this is also much more hands on. Yes, you can hire a general contractor, but you'll need to be on site frequently to confirm the work is being done to your specifications and on time.

I personally love real estate. I love flipping properties and do most of the work myself, but it is time-consuming. You've got to be committed to your properties.

Renting

The driver of many real estate investors is the monthly rent they receive from tenants. When it comes to renting, you can purchase residential or commercial properties.

Real estate comes down to location. Understanding the area and the type of people who live in that area gives you a great indication of the type of tenant you will find.

Find a real estate agent who can find great deals. A good deal is buying below market value. This gives you more profit when you sell.

As you continue to buy rental properties, you'll increase your understanding of what a 'good deal' is. This takes time and experience. For example, a good deal in one area might not be a good deal in your area. Every city and block are different. There are nuances you will never understand until you spend time there. A great real estate agent will help but don't leave all the work up to her. Do your own research. Visit the areas you want to buy in. This is your investment.

I didn't understand what it meant to do this research when I bought the duplex. I overpaid for it and tried to rent in an area that didn't attract the best tenants. These were mistakes I made. Luckily, it didn't cost me too much in the end.

I learned a ton about real estate through this duplex experience. I realized how important the location is and how important doing research is. This made all four of my flipping experiences favorable.

Flipping

If you decide flipping real estate is for you, build a skill at finding the deals. You can use foreclosure auctions, contacts at your local bank, wholesale contacts, and other real estate contacts to find deals. Build relationships with these people. They are closer to the supply and can point you in the right direction. Depending on how long you own the flip property, there may not be much organic appreciation in the value of the property, but your renovations should add a significant amount of appreciation to its value.

After you've renovated the property, you have two options. You can sell it immediately or you can rent it out. If you sell it immediately, you've just given yourself a windfall of cash on the sale, especially if you paid all cash for the property originally. Having cash frees you up to do another flip or allows you to enjoy a well-deserved break. The con is depending on how you set up your flipping business, you'll likely pay ordinary income tax on this profit.

The alternative is renting your flip after you've done the renovation. The pros to this are monthly passive income for as long as you rent the property and no immediate tax hit. If your primary business is renting, and you hold onto the property for at least one year, then you would be able to take advantage of the capital gains rate, which is lower than your ordinary income rate. The cons to renting are you don't get your initial cash investment or profit from the appreciation back immediately. You'll earn additional rents, but the big cash windfall won't be received until you sell the property. The other con is tenants may tear up the work you've put into this property. They likely won't treat it as well as someone who owns it.

Moving Primary Residence

Another strategy for real estate is flipping your primary residence. You may not have considered this as a path to wealth, but I know many people who have used this strategy successfully. There is a tax loophole that allows the profit you make from the sale of your primary residence to be tax-free. That's right, if you sell your home for $100,000 more than you purchased for and you've lived in the property for at least two years of the last five years, you don't pay income taxes on that $100,000. Gains up to $250,000 per person are not taxable. This means, if you profited $270,000 on your property and your filing status is single, then you would only pay taxes on a $20,000 gain. If you're married filing jointly, you can gain up to $500,000 without a tax consequence.

My dad worked with a guy who owned a construction company. He moved his family about every three to five years to take advantage of this. His wife wasn't as excited about it as he was, but they became very wealthy through these moves. I know another woman who took jobs in different parts of the US at various times. Her and her husband purchased a new property in the new location each time. Every time they sold the last property, they earned a great deal of non-taxable profit.

This is the best strategy if you don't want to flip multiple properties every year and you also don't want to be a landlord. How bothered would you be to move every three to five years? This is an easy way to make money in real estate and avoid income taxes. If you want to learn more about this loophole, go to the IRS website (irs.gov) and read Publication 523.

Leaping into Businesses

If you aren't attracted to real estate or stock investments, owning a business might be the appreciating asset for you.

Businesses come in all shapes and sizes, from someone owning a retail store to someone working from home providing services on the Internet. Businesses include both tangible products and intangible services. Businesses generate a wide range of revenues and margins, based on the market of those products and services.

There are many ways to acquire a business. You can start one from scratch. You can buy an existing business. You can purchase a franchise. Or you can buy into a business as a partial owner.

When it comes to businesses, the opportunities are endless. If you have a particular skill, it makes sense to go in that direction. For example, you may be an excellent carpenter, electrician, plumber, real estate agent, lawyer, accountant, dentist, marketer, chiropractor, writer, coach, etc. Many of these occupations start their own businesses at some point in their careers. You may plan to be an owner-operator in the short-term, but have a long-term vision to build a team, giving you more freedom.

The pros for this type of business are you understand the business well. You've already developed the skills around this type of work, and it's your business; you own 100% of it. No one is going to tell you how to run it. The cons are it's going to take work to get off the ground and time to create a solid customer base as well as a brand and reputation.

Franchising is another avenue within the business category. Have you ever searched for franchise opportunities? Many of us think of restaurants when we hear franchise, but they come in many different industries from travel agencies to movers, home care, signs production and sports academies.

The pros of a franchise are the proven business model and existing template for you to follow. The cons are you've got to abide by someone else's rules, and it costs money to purchase the rights to the franchise. You'll pay an initial investment fee as well as recurring royalties.

Another way to invest in businesses is to become a partner. Partnerships can be risky, because you are relying on your partners' continued interest in the business, but they can be powerful as well. Some businesses are too large for one person to purchase, but with the combined investments, it makes the acquisition possible. Think about a minor league baseball team or a real estate development. It's common for multiple people to go in on these businesses together.

The pros are you aren't taking on all the risk, these can be lucrative investments, and you can learn a lot from your partners, especially if they have more experience than you. The cons are you will not have full control. In other words, your vote may not count for much. And these generally require large investments.

There are endless opportunities to allow your money to grow as you've seen in this chapter. The key is to pick something you enjoy. Choose something that complements your skills. And select the appreciating assets you can see yourself still loving in 10 years. Many of these assets don't provide amazing returns in one year. To get the bang for your buck, you need to commit for at least 5 years.

Action 15 – Calculate When You Will Become Financially Free

Nothing is more inspiring than having a target for when you gain complete control of your time. In other words, you're financially free and able to do exactly what you want to do. When you get to this point, you can retire, you can keep working, you can take time off, you can find a part-time job, and you can volunteer. It doesn't matter what you do; you've accumulated enough assets to not only cover your expenses, but also to allow you to continue investing.

A few years ago, when I became more serious about retiring early, I put together this spreadsheet. This gave me the target of retiring in 2025. I'm three years into this, and my numbers are off. I have slightly less in retirement, much more in non-income generating real estate, and less in stock investments. This isn't a hard line for you to stick to, but it gives you guidance for future decisions.

401k

Year	Beg Bal	return 5%	contribution 33,880	end bal
2020	$ 312,000			$ 312,000
2021	$ 422,000			$ 422,000
2022	$ 569,000	$ 28,450	$ 33,880	$ 631,330
2023	$ 631,330	$ 31,567	$ 33,880	$ 696,777
2024	$ 696,777	$ 34,839	$ 33,880	$ 765,495
2025	$ 765,495	$ 38,275	$ 33,880	$ 837,650
2026	$ 837,650	$ 41,883		$ 879,533
2027	$ 879,531	$ 43,977		$ 923,509
2028	$ 923,509	$ 46,175		$ 969,685
2029	$ 969,685	$ 48,484		$ 1,018,169
2030	$ 1,018,169	$ 50,908		$ 1,069,077
2031	$ 1,069,077	$ 53,454		$ 1,122,531
2032	$ 1,122,531	$ 56,127		$ 1,178,658
2033	$ 1,178,658	$ 58,933		$ 1,237,591
2034	$ 1,237,591	$ 61,880		$ 1,299,470
2035	$ 1,299,470	$ 64,974		$ 1,364,444
2036	$ 1,364,444	$ 68,222		$ 1,432,666
2037	$ 1,432,666	$ 71,633		$ 1,504,299
2038	$ 1,504,299	$ 75,215		$ 1,579,514
2039	$ 1,579,514	$ 78,976		$ 1,658,490

Brokerage account

Year	Beg Bal	return 5%	contribution 36,000	withdraw	end bal
2020	$ 150,000				$ 150,000
2021	$ 170,000				$ 170,000
2022	$ 200,000	$ 10,000	$ 36,000		$ 246,000
2023	$ 246,000	$ 12,300	$ 36,000		$ 294,300
2024	$ 294,300	$ 14,715	$ 36,000		$ 345,015
2025	$ 345,015	$ 17,251	$ 36,000		$ 398,266
2026	$ 398,266	$ 19,913		$(40,000)	$ 378,179
2027	$ 378,179	$ 18,909		$(40,000)	$ 357,088
2028	$ 357,088	$ 17,854		$(40,000)	$ 334,942
2029	$ 334,942	$ 16,747		$(40,000)	$ 311,690
2030	$ 311,690	$ 15,584		$(40,000)	$ 287,274
2031	$ 287,274	$ 14,364		$(40,000)	$ 261,638
2032	$ 261,638	$ 13,082		$(40,000)	$ 234,720
2033	$ 234,720	$ 11,736		$(40,000)	$ 206,456
2034	$ 206,456	$ 10,323		$(40,000)	$ 176,778
2035	$ 176,778	$ 8,839		$(40,000)	$ 145,617
2036	$ 145,617	$ 7,281		$(40,000)	$ 112,898
2037	$ 112,898	$ 5,645		$(40,000)	$ 78,543
2038	$ 78,543	$ 3,927		$(40,000)	$ 42,470
2039	$ 42,470	$ 2,124		$(40,000)	$ 4,594

Recall, your retirement value is the point where your investments generate enough passive income for you to live off them. For simplicity, I used $40,000, which you can see in the withdraw column. I could comfortably live off $40,000 a year if I never moved. I live in a low-cost area and have no debt. The caveat is I can't touch my retirement until age 59 and a half, therefore the balance in the 401k section isn't accessible until 2039.

After 2025 I won't have to contribute another penny to my 401k. It will naturally continue to compound, and if it grows at 5% (which is very conservative), I'll have over $1,600,000 when I'm able to withdraw from this account.

The right side shows my non-retirement balance. This is the scarier piece. Again, I was conservative and only assumed a 5% return. If I stop contributing to this account in 2025 with almost $400,000 and withdraw $40,000 each year, I will have enough to cover all the years until I turn 59 and a half.

This is cutting it too close though. I can't retire knowing that at age 59 I might only have $4,000 in this account. I do plan to retire from my corporate job at some point, but I don't plan on stopping my income.

The first action I took after seeing these numbers was figuring out how to make more passive income. It's a puzzle. I know I need to earn $3,500 per month to live comfortably. How do I create that income? When you see these questions as puzzles, you'll end up with many ideas to tackle your dilemma. I'm still in the process of figuring this out, but the foundation is there. I know how much I need to earn. I've already solved part of the puzzle.

Create this for yourself. How much do you want to spend each year? This is based on your projected expenses and desired investment contributions. Whatever this number is, work backwards to figure out how much you need to have invested. Let's say your number is $40,000 as well. And let's assume you're going to use the 4% withdraw rule.

This is similar to the retirement target exercise we did in Chapter 10. However, in this example, you are refining the calculation. Here you are separating your retirement balance from your non-retirement balance.

If your target annual income was $40,000, then you would need $1,000,000 in investments to create that passive income. But, what if your $1,000,000 was 100% in retirement accounts and you wanted to retire at age 50? With a few exceptions, you wouldn't have access to your retirement accounts until age 59 and a half. In this calculation you can differentiate between retirement investments and non-retirement investments. You can run different scenarios to see how much you would need in non-retirement accounts to retire early.

With these exercises you're refining your vision of financial freedom. You're breaking down your big targets into daily actions. The more transparency you have in your money, the more refined your plan can be.

16: Stay the Course

You now have a mindset that tells you you're going to be a millionaire. You're going to pay off your debt. You're going to become financially free.

I want to brace you though. After I paid off my debt, there were months where I felt unmotivated. $1,000,000 is a large number. 10 years might seem like a quick trip to becoming a millionaire, but when you're in the middle of it and you don't see progress for months because the market is down, it's easy to lose your motivation.

This is why it's important to build your investment muscle. Many employers automatically withdraw your retirement contributions each paycheck. Many discount brokerages allow you to set up auto-withdraws for your non-retirement investing. When you consistently invest each paycheck, even when the market is red, you are building your investment muscle. To create a stronger muscle, you must condition it.

Another mindset trick is understanding what's really happening when the market is heading downward. When the market is red, remember, you can buy more shares with the same amount cash. Let's say you invest $500 of every paycheck. The index fund you bought was $100 last week, meaning you bought 5 shares, but this week it's down to $75. This means you can buy 6.7 shares for that same $500. It's not always a bad thing when the market turns. If you were to go to the grocery store, and everything was on sale at 25% off, you would be excited. However, for some reason when we see stock prices on sale, we get scared.

I completely understand this perspective though. When you're tracking your net worth each paycheck or each month, you are looking at your total and your trend. You are still working hard at your job, but your total net worth isn't growing. I know this feeling. Focus on the fact that you are purchasing more shares for less and those shares are going to be worth much more in the future.

Myth 16: Success Happens Overnight

When you see someone's success, know that you are only seeing the tip of the iceberg.

It took almost 5 years to pay off my debt. It took a full year to gain traction on my blog. It took me 5 months to get more than eleven X (formerly Twitter) followers. Success never happens overnight. It takes repeated, consistent actions over time to make real progress. For those months when my X account wasn't attracting many followers, I kept posting every day. I kept improving my writing and trying to understand how best to add value for my readers. No one, including you or me, has all the knowledge when we start. That's why it's important to start small habits and let them build up over time.

You will continue to refine your mindset throughout the rest of your life. You're not going to change everything in two weeks. It doesn't matter if you pull all-nighters and work intensely for the next two weeks. You're not going to solve your money problems that quickly. You can make progress in two weeks, but you can't solve everything.

Anyone you look up to today who represents being successful in your mind once had to start somewhere. They weren't born with 100,000 followers. They weren't born the CEO of a large company. Many weren't born a celebrity. They worked and failed and tried different approaches. They learned every time an approach didn't work. That is what separates many people today. Some people are willing to take that risk and fail in front of others, while others aren't willing to fail.

Too many of us try one approach and if it doesn't work, we quit. That will never make you successful. When you start something new, how do you expect to know everything you need to know? Experience and failure are what teach you the lessons to improve on your next try. It's the people who are willing to try that come out on top. Those happen to be the same people that fail the most.

Life really is trial and error. Try and see if it works. If it doesn't, at least you learned something new. Either try a different approach or try something else.

Action 16 – Find Inspiration Daily

It's easy to get inspired temporarily by reading a book, attending a conference, or going to a corporate training. I've been to many workshops provided by my companies. During these trainings many ideas come to my mind, and I feel inspired to make changes. Then, without fail, I go back to my desk surrounded by my colleagues, and there I am, no longer feeling those inspired thoughts I had just the day before. What happened? Where did they go?

This isn't uncommon. It's easy to feel inspired one minute and then back to default mode the next. When you go back to the same environment with the same people and same habits, it's hard to keep that level of motivation. To avoid this, find something that inspires you every day. I use multiple things, but a lot of my daily inspiration comes from podcasts. By listening to speakers who are inspiring, I consistently find those feelings. I've been listening to some podcasts for years now, and it's only in the last year I realized why I was still listening to those same podcasts. I do it to stay inspired.

People often say motivation doesn't last. Well, neither does bathing – that's why we recommend it daily. – Zig Ziglar

Find something that inspires you each day. Is it reading a book, listening to a podcast, or watching a television program? It doesn't need to be the same thing every day. There is no one-size-fits-all for inspiration. Find what makes you smile and what makes you work harder. Maybe it's seeing your kids before they go to school or talking to your parents.

To achieve your goals, especially the big ones, it's imperative you stay inspired. Find something that inspires you every day. You need it.

Without it, it's easy to give into the negative thoughts or the monotonousness of the days. Be a guardian to the external influences that get into your mind. You already know how important your thoughts are. Don't let external influences add negativity to your mind. Don't let the news or the opinions of your surrounding family and friends get past your filters.

Put your 'why' in a place where you see it every day. Maybe it's a photo of your family or a photo of your dream. Your 'why' is the reason you're working so hard. Keep it in a visible spot.

Be a Life-Long Learner

Millionaires never stop learning. The funny thing about learning is the more you learn, the more you realize you don't know. As we open our minds to new perspectives, we see how many other perspectives there are. We understand topics from different angles. We gain insights.

I read a lot of non-fiction books. In many cases, I understand the topic, but the author puts a slight twist on the topic which makes me think differently about it. It's those slight twists that keep me learning. Those slivers of new insight can be the catalyst of an amazing idea. This is why I read so much. I get great ideas from books. I see things in a new light.

Too many people go through life accepting the situations they're in. They assume their current circumstances are permanent. They become accustomed to their job, their environment, and their habits, and they don't want to change. They've created a world that works for them with limits all around them, so they stop trying. They stop learning.

Don't be this person. Don't be the person that sets limits in your mind and lives by those limits. Set your sight higher. Know that your current situation is only temporary, and there is a big world out there with a million different perspectives and many million people. You have the power to create a new life if you keep learning and keep your eyes open.

If I had accepted my circumstances from childhood as my permanent way of life, I would have missed so much. I would be living paycheck to paycheck, most likely working at a job I didn't like and barely making much money. Instead, I chose a different path.

You shouldn't accept your current circumstances either. Find a way out. Take a risk. You might fail, but you will learn so much in the process. I took a risk. I moved across the country. I took out too much debt. I made a lot of mistakes. However, I never gave up. I never quit on my big picture.

Celebrate the Small Wins

Life is about enjoying the small things. When your spouse cooks an amazing meal, when your child falls asleep on your lap, and when the sun is shining are just a few examples. If you can't find appreciation in the small things, this life is going to be difficult. The more goodness we recognize each day, the better our life feels.

Celebrate the small things. Celebration can be a source of inspiration. BJ Fogg introduced this concept in his book, *Tiny Habits*. Every time you complete a habit that is hard for you, even if it's just accomplishing a small piece of the habit, celebrate. Cheer for yourself.

I do this while I'm running. I'm not a natural runner, and even though it has become easier, it's still hard. Once I make it through a mile, I give myself a cheer. I think about how healthy it is and how much stronger my body feels. That helps me get through the next two miles. It works too. Every time you push yourself out of your comfort zone, give yourself a cheer. Be enthusiastic; you have accomplished something, and that is something to be happy about.

Cheering yourself makes you feel good inside. No longer allow any negative self-talk. With all the negative external influences, you don't need to add to this negativity. Say positive things to yourself. Not only will this make you feel better, but it will make you want to tackle more. When you cheer yourself, you will more likely finish what you start, whether it's exercising, giving a speech, studying, eating healthier, paying off your debt or getting your job done well.

You're an expert now. You have all the knowledge to become a millionaire. By following these 5 stages of money, you are on your way.

Notes

Gillespie, Lane. (2023). Average American Debt Statistics. Page 48. https://www.bankrate.com/personal-finance/debt/average-american-debt/

Bourne, Jenny, and Rosenmerkel, Lisa. Over the Top: How Tax Returns Show that the Very Rich are Different from You and Me. Page 169. https://www.irs.gov/pub/irs-soi/14rpoverthetopbournerosenmerkel.pdf

www.ingramcontent.com/pod-product-compliance
Lightning Source LLC
Chambersburg PA
CBHW070527200326
41519CB00013B/2959